100 Ideas for Secondary Teachers

Outstanding Lessons

Ross Morrison McGill

BLOOMS

Published 2013 by Bloomsbury Education

Bloomsbury Publishing plc

50 Bedford Square, London, WC1B 3DP

www.bloomsbury.com

978-1-4729-0530-7

A CIP record for this publication is available from the British Library.

3 5 7 9 10 8 6 4

Typeset by Fakenham Prepress Solutions, Fakenham, Norfolk, NR21 8NN

Printed and bound by CPI Group (UK) Ltd, Croydon, CR0 4YY

This book is produced using paper that is made from wood grown in managed, sustainable forests. It is natural, renewable and recyclable. The logging and manufacturing processes conform to the environmental regulations of the country of origin.

To view more of our titles please visit www.bloomsbury.com

Online resources accompany this book available at:
www.bloomsbury.com/TeacherToolkit

Please type the URL into your web browser and follow the instructions to access the resources. If you experience any problems, please contact Bloomsbury at: companionwebsite@bloomsbury.com

Senior leadership redundancy was a blessing. With no job, marooned 85 miles from home, facing 82 days in hospital, my resilient, wee schoolboy @FreddieWM was born. From then on I started writing seriously, witnessing human strength, at its most fervent, yet delicate.

This book was tough, but not as hard-hitting as May 2011. This is for you @JenniMcGill and our pint-sized gift from God.

Other titles in the 100 Ideas for Secondary Teachers series:

100 Ideas for Secondary Teachers: Managing Behaviour by Johnnie Young

100 Ideas for Secondary Teachers: Gifted and Talented by John Senior

Other Secondary titles available from Bloomsbury Education:

How to Survive your First Year in Teaching by Sue Cowley

Teacher: Mastering the Art and Craft of Teaching by Tom Bennett

Why Are You Shouting At Us? by Phil Beadle and John Murphy

Contents

Acknowledgements

I would like to express recognition to the following super-teachers who have presented an idea for this book. They are contemporaries I know personally, either physically, digitally via Twitter, or both. As a direct result, may I introduce you to the conceptualisation of #Challabing.

challabing, verb.

Pronunciation: tʃæˈlæbɪŋ
Etymology: **chap**ter + colla**b**orations.
Definition: to collaborate on the creation of a chapter or idea.

Guest authors:

Idea 16: Hayley Thompson: @HThompson1982
www.educatingmatters.wordpress.com

Ideas 20, 28 and 68: Stephen Tierney: @LeadingLearner
www.leadinglearner.me

Idea 25: Moheeni Patel: @MoheeniPatel
www.moheenipatel.wordpress.com/

Idea 54: Christopher Waugh: @Edutronic_Net
www.chris.edutronic.net

Idea 64: Stephen Lockyer: @MrLockyer
www.classroomtm.co.uk

Idea 75: Sarah Findlater: @MsFindlater
www.msfindlater.blogspot.co.uk

Idea 86: Ian McDaid: @IanMcDaid
www.sleramblings.wordpress.com

With references to:

Idea 29: David Didau: @LearningSpy – www.learningspy.co.uk

Idea 64: John Sayers: @JohnSayers – http://sayersjohn.blogspot.co.uk

Idea 77: Keven Bartle: @KevBartle – www.dailygenius.wordpress.com

Idea 100: Mark Anderson: @ICTEvangelist – http://ictevangelist.com

Secondly, I'd like to acknowledge my (PLN) Professional Learning Network. Without your critique and interest, none of this would be possible. To the individuals that I work (or have worked) with; the people

I follow on Twitter and to the thousands of you who choose to follow me. If we have shared a tweet or two, a staffroom gossip or some corridor-banter, then thank you for the dialogue.

Blogging professionally has led to the production of this book, so I do hope that it will inspire many more educators to be open and reflective online. I am confident that professional-blogging will be recognised and acceptable CPD in the near future; so inherently established, that it becomes part of every teacher's bloodstream. It's free, powered with wonderful and inspirational people. So, get blogging!

Finally, a colossal box of chocolates to Holly Gardner and Jen Seth at Bloomsbury Publishing for all your encouragement and sublime editing skills.

Introduction

More than ever, we need formidable and first-class practitioners in our classrooms. It takes an outstanding teacher to inspire the next generation of teachers and Mr Paul Boldy (Fleetwood High School c.1990) was mine, who inspired me to step into teaching when I was just 18 years old! It was one of the best decisions I ever made.

This book is literally my teaching-brain, wrenched open and placed under the microscope for all to see! Full of my top-drawer ideas, I'm confident you will find many to suit your own subject.

This book is easy-going and can be used in a potluck fashion, or more thoughtfully. Many ideas are selected so that you can pick and prepare them just five minutes before a lesson. Some ideas require no planning whatsoever and for me, that's what makes it a marvel to read for those with little time on their hands.

The sections are separated into typical teaching and learning topics so you can effortlessly hunt for an idea. They have been carefully matched to suit the latest criteria for 'Outstanding' teaching.

I have judiciously selected a small group of outstanding teachers I collaborate with, physically and digitally. I highly recommend that you put this book down and look them up immediately! They have provided superb ideas in this book and blog regularly online.

This book is also full of hashtags and hyperlinks to the web and to various people on Twitter. This has been premeditated to encourage reflective pedagogy, promote teacher-distant-collaboration and the universal contribution of classroom ideas. It will be interesting to observe how some of you take the ideas on and push them forward.

I encourage you to share what you are doing with each of the ideas, using the book's main hashtag, #100Ideas, or where there is a specific chapter-hashtag with me at @TeacherToolkit.

"There are many roads to Outstanding."
Ross

How to use this book

Teaching tip

A little bit of extra advice on how or how not to run the activity or put the strategy into practice.

Taking it further

Makes a suggestion for you to consider taking the idea a little further than I have written in the book. It perhaps will take longer to implement, but will make the idea all the more richer. If you choose to use any of these, please share the results with everyone via #100Ideas.

Bonus idea   ★

Are rare and occasionally, off-the-wall nuggets. I've shared these very wisely as I will be left with nothing in the tank to keep you interested online...!

#100Ideas

This book includes quick, easy, practical ideas for you to dip in and out of, in order to move your practice in the classroom from 'good' to 'outstanding'.

Each idea includes:

- A catchy title, easy to refer to and share with your colleagues
- An opening quote – either an extract from the Ofsted observation framework, used when observing 'Outstanding' teaching, or a quirky interesting quote to catch your attention!
- A summary of the idea in bold, making it easy to flick through the book and identify an idea you want to use at a glance
- A step-by-step guide to implementing the idea.

Each idea also includes one or more of the following and the features in the margin:

Hashtags and links to Twitter. I have created hashtags for some ideas, so that you can follow what everyone else is achieving with the same idea online and in real-time. This will allow the debate to continue with others and also evolve and endorse each idea.

Online resources also accompany this book. When the link to the resource is referenced in the book, logon to www.bloomsbury.com/TeacherToolkit to find the extra resources, catalogued under the relevant idea number.

Starts of lessons

Part 1

Snappy starters

"Outstanding lessons are well judged and imaginative teaching strategies are often used."

The importance of having a snappy starter is fundamental for getting lessons off to a great start. It ensures students are focused from the outset and routines and expectations are established.

I advise you to choose five of your best ideas to use each half term and stick with them. Deliver the starters each week and then rotate the content slightly to suit a new topic or group.

- Snowball – spelling test; scrunch up paper, throw across room, unravel, correct any misspellings, add a word and throw on.
- Broken/fix it – place a text, object or a project on the table and ask students to repair.
- Provoking images – to stir a debate or guess who/what/why?
- Puzzled – turn images into jigsaws and piece together at www.jigsawplanet.com or www.puzz-it.com.
- Pandora's box – contains mysterious contents and clues.

One of my favourite resources for engaging starters is Triptico, a simple desktop application for your computer. Triptico allows you to quickly create interactive learning resources to use in your classroom. Designed and created by David Riley, they can be modified to suit any subject, any age and degree of learning. Grab yours here: www.triptico.co.uk. There are many resources on there including team scores; word magnets; timers and countdowns; group and question selectors. This will help to get those run-of-the-mill lessons, starting with quirky strategies and tingling-inspired teaching.

The first words

"Pencils out!"

As each student enters the room, deliver your first instruction to engage and focus the students immediately on something simple and explicit.

I always deliver my first instruction outside the classroom door. This is rarely delivered to the whole class at once, but is often directed one-to-one as each student enters the room. Not only is this a simple way to welcome each student or revisit progress from the previous lesson, but it also gives you the opportunity to ensure that every child hears and acts on your first instruction. It should be a bite-sized chunk of information that ensures that no matter what happens next, the primary goal is to achieve something simple before the lesson can begin. It is usually something unassuming that requires minimal listening skills. Combining it with a visual clue often encourages students to settle down more quickly during the physical combat of bags, jackets, planners, pencils cases and text books! The instruction can be as simple as 'pencils out' whilst holding a pencil so that lessons can get off to a prompt start.

My top five first instructions:

1 Pencils (or pens) out!
2 Right, let's go!
3 I want to tell you a secret...
4 Read; think; write; share.
5 I challenge you to...

Taking it further

Provide incentives for students who follow your instructions without the need for a verbal cue. Turn the first five minutes of your lesson into a silent movie and encourage all your lessons to start calmly and intuitively.

The whiteboard says it all

"I even have one stitched to the fabric of my apron!"

Multifunctional, versatile and so handy, mini whiteboards are all the rage.

You will find mini whiteboards everywhere in schools these days. They are incorporated into the pages at the back of student and teacher planners; there will be a complete set of A4 boards, one for each student, shoehorned into a plastic box at the side of the teacher's desk. They are everywhere!

Before mini whiteboards became vogue in all classrooms, I was 'Whiteboard King' in a school many moons ago! You'd always find a mini whiteboard in my hand, one screwed to the outside of my classroom door, one on the back of my teacher planner, one in my office and even stitched to the fabric of my workshop apron! Mini whiteboards in the hands of a teacher can be used for the following purposes, along with many others:

1 Providing whole-class demonstrations; writing up keywords or figures.
2 Signalling key phrases to the class. For example: three minutes left; plenary time; working in pairs; collect feedback; investigate etc.
3 Mini whiteboards can help solve problems with students one-on-one, or in small groups around a table, without the need to stop the whole class from working.

Routines!

"It's all about the routines."

There is a clear stipulation in the Ofsted framework that lessons should have routines that are evident, so make sure you remember: routines, routines, routines!

Routines start from outside the classroom door. Setting expectations from the outset is paramount for getting lessons off to a good start. Get off your chair! Meet and greet your students at the door. Have those initial conversations: say hello, welcome. It all contributes to a positive ethos for high standards. Evidence from observations and student conversations can inform you of what a typical lesson is really like, from simply lining up outside, to classroom activities such as peer assessment and group presentations. If students expect this to be the norm at the start of your lesson, then they will be expectant from lesson to lesson.

Routines for the start of your lessons:

- Be on time to lessons.
- Meet and greet your students at the door.
- Place one foot in the classroom and one foot in the corridor.
- Speak! Saying something as simple as 'welcome' to every student can make all the difference.
- If the entrance to the classroom is not calm and quiet, DO IT AGAIN!
- Do not be afraid to repeat simple processes to ensure they become the norm. Sweat the small stuff!

Teaching tip

I often tell students that I feel like a record-player when setting expectations and re-capping on routines. Rather than repeating instructions time and time again until you are blue in the face, consider using keywords or symbols on your classroom wall. It not only saves your voice, but also provides visual clues, that you can point to. Take a look at my reminder poster online at www.bloomsbury.com/ TeacherToolkit and read Idea 14.

Monday morning mantra (MMM)

"When you're smiling, when you're smiling, the whole world smiles with you... But when you're crying, you bring on the rain, so stop your sighing, be happy again!"

Whether it is Monday morning or Friday afternoon, you should be smiling. Follow my Monday morning mantra and smile today!

There were never truer words spoken than those in the lyrics of the song above. My own personal challenge is to live up to these words on a Monday morning, period one with Year 9. Students know instinctively if you are in a good or a bad mood and I know that I, quite possibly, appear less positive and generous first thing on a Monday than I would do on a Friday! No matter what strategy I employ on a Sunday evening, I always find myself a little bleary-eyed when retuning to the classroom the next day. So, I have developed a Monday morning mantra to ensure my Monday lessons get off to a great start!

- **M: Music** works wonders. Any rhythm can help to revitalise attitudes to learning.
- **O: Original thinking** doesn't always have to be new. Keep ideas relevant and current.
- **N: Noise level and pitch** is vital for energetic or calming lessons.
- **D: Demotivated learning** should be banned. Avoid tests, copying and worksheets!
- **A: Always smile**. It really does work and no matter how tired or moody you are feeling, a simple smile will brighten up your day and could potentially change a student's outlook.
- **Y: Yes, yes, yes!** Challenge yourself to say 'yes' when questions are asked. This will ultimately lead to you and your students taking more risks.

Taking it further

I dare you to suggest MMM to a colleague who is infamous for having a glum face! The next time they complain about student behaviour, tell them to smile and then tweet 'smile' to #100MMM!

#100MMM

The face that says it all

"I can pull all sorts of funny faces. I'm particularly dexterous with my eyebrows!"

Stand in front of a mirror and practise your upset face or a cold glare; you know, the one that stops students in their tracks and requires no verbal accompaniment.

Get your lessons off to an engaging start. Proclaim to the class, 'I wasn't going to tell you this and I'm not sure the time is right, but...' before introducing a provocative image, a movie, a news item or a resource that is linked to their learning to stir a debate. Make sure your face says it all.

I'm a huge believer in teaching for dramatic effect. The more expressive and engaging we are as individuals, the more we can captivate our students. Have you ever watched other colleagues and marvelled at how they can reduce an assembly room full of rowdy Year 11s to silence on a hot and sweaty Friday afternoon? I have, it can be mesmerising. But, how do you bottle this and use it yourself? The next time you notice this happening, watch the teacher's facial expressions. Look very carefully at their eyes; their eyebrows; listen to their choice of language, as well as their body language, positioning and movement. How would you describe it?

Try incorporating some of these strategies into your own teaching to ensure lessons get off to a dramatic start!

Taking it further

Ask a Drama teacher to help you set up a role play by visiting your classroom and delivering some good or bad news to you, or the class. Or visit your Drama department and watch them teach. How do they use their voice, their body, their face to deliver engaging instructions?

Corridor chaos

"Be aware of not just the physical intruders, but the auditory, aromatic and invisible ones too."

Noisy corridors don't need you screaming down the hallways too! Grab a small whiteboard, a pen and an engaging object. Write down a simple question for students to think about in return for a reward.

If you are in the habit of meeting and greeting every group of students as they arrive you will be familiar with the importance of standing at your classroom door. Unfortunately, you might also be familiar with other, unexpected factors that might be lurking outside your classroom: busy, claustrophobic corridors, noisy conversations, excruciatingly loud school bells, odd smells. A myriad of other factors can easily drift into the classroom and affect your students' moods and the general atmosphere. Without doubt, how you deal with these external influences can either get your lesson off to an outstanding or an inadequate start!

Here are my top five strategies to maintain a great start off the corridor:

1 Trooping the colour! Absolute military precision. Insist on silence and one shoulder against the wall. Planners and pens out. Jackets off. Repeat to each student one by one as you walk the line.
2 Consider meeting your students at a different location.
3 Hand out engaging information as each student lines up.
4 Get into character. Don a costume or adopt an unexpected persona.
5 Stand halfway down the class line, rather than just at the front. Have something visual in your hand to gain their attention.

#CorridorChaos

Get spiked!

"The most failsafe way to create a learning buzz."

Feeling a bit prickly? Kids getting you all worked up? Start your lessons off with a few prongs, pricks and prods. Get spiked!

You should always be looking for any opportunity to create a 'spike' for students to be engaged. The spike is a catch or hook on learning. The most failsafe way to create a learning buzz in a classroom is by giving students a leadership role to work on finding a solution to a posed problem. Other ideas include:

- Invite another teacher into your classroom, someone who is typically known for being of a specific disposition, stern perhaps, and pre-plan a short drama to set the scene for the lesson. Ask your Drama department to help you out.
- Ask students to take on a new identity for the lesson: a detective, a politician, maybe even the teacher!
- Place a provocative image on the interactive whiteboard as students arrive. Include an instruction so students can start without your direction. For example, Why might this image upset you? Use the image to generate discussion.
- Provide a pack of information containing a jigsaw; some flashcards, or a map with clues.
- Stick masking tape around the shape of your body on the floor (you will need help!) and leave learning clues with numbered markers around the scene.

Teaching tip

The planning for such an activity requires a great deal of thinking. Whatever you decide to do, the fundamental principle is that students are captured by the message from the outset and are left to explore and lead their own learning. At all costs, avoid teacher talk from the start and create opportunities for students to lead and get spiked!

Taking it further

Set out your intent from the start. Inform students that you are only allowed to say 'yes' or 'no'. This will encourage students to fire questions at you and lead to spiked learning and risk taking.

#GetSpiked

9

Planning

Part 2

The five minute lesson plan

"Yes! You really can plan a lesson in five minutes!"

Print and scribble your way to Outstanding with the five minute lesson plan.

The five minute lesson plan reduces planning time, but also improves your lesson planning and delivery. It allows you to focus on the key elements of a lesson and enables progress to be identified in your planning, therefore increasing the potential for outstanding judgments.

The template can be used at any stage of your career and for any occasion. I have used it for many formal observations, as well as unplanned Ofsted inspections with great success. It has also been highly successful when coaching new teachers or helping those who require improvement. The popularity of the plan has even been evidenced in a recent Ofsted report!

Download your own five minute lesson plan template online at: www.bloomsbury.com/ TeacherToolkit and refer to it whilst reading the description below.

How it works:

1 **The big picture**: How does the lesson fit into your scheme of work? What knowledge will your students enter the classroom with already? Describe the lesson in 30 seconds!
2 **Objectives**: What are the objectives for the lesson? Try to incorporate at least two different levelled objectives – perhaps allow students to choose their own.
3 **Engagement**: What's the catch? How will you gain student attention at the start and throughout the lesson? Will it be exciting and meaningful? Is it enough to entice students into learning? It's not needed every lesson, but a good story is often enough!

4 **Stickability**: What will stick in students' minds as they leave your lesson? What key points do you want them to remember and bring back to the next lesson?

5 **Assessment for Learning (AfL)**: How will you assess how your learners are getting on during the lesson so that you know how to take them where you want to go? What AfL strategies are you going to use? Plan various AfL strategies that will allow students to see their own progress.

6 **Key words**: Literacy has never had such a high profile as it has at the moment. Encourage students to read lesson objectives aloud. Pick out keywords and extrapolate their meanings. Use techniques to break down the phonics of each word and encourage visual recognition to reinforce. Plan which keyword you want your students to learn. This promotes high levels of literacy, which is an Ofsted focus.

7 **Differentiation**: Plan which activities you will provide for gifted and talented students, students with Special Educational Needs and Disabilities (SEN/D) and students with English as an Additional Language (EAL). What sort of groupings are needed, what are they doing and when? Do you have this mapped to a seating plan with current levels of progress?

8 **Learning episodes**: What is going to happen in the lesson from start to finish? Identify as many opportunities for student-led learning as possible. The four boxes on the template do not denote a four part lesson, just fill them up with what needs to happen.

This format was shared with me by John Bayley and has since been modified. It is incredibly popular on Twitter and the TES Resource website. Don't be shy. Start using it today and if you're feeling brave, post a photo of your lesson plan on Twitter for all other subject teachers to use or tweak.

Taking it further

If you want to take this further you can try Idea 86, the five minute evaluation plan for reflecting on your lesson plan and the lesson itself. It can be downloaded online at: www.bloomsbury.com/TeacherToolkit. There are also many subject specific versions and translated language versions on the TES and via my website. Find out more: www.bit.ly/More5MinPlan

Bonus idea ★

Get students to plan their own lessons by providing a large A3 laminated copy of the five minute lesson plan. You may need to change some of the headings to suit the context of your school or subject.

#5MinPlan

Smarter marking

"What? Why? How?"

It's all about saving time and, at the same time, improving quality. Is this truly possible? Teach your students to become smarter assessors and save time on marking and giving feedback.

#SmartAss

To improve students' understanding of their own work, I embed this simple questioning strategy in their feedback; they spend three minutes reporting '**What** they have done, **Why** they have done it, and **How** they did it.' I get my students to record this in a speech bubble that can often be a doodle on the page. Below are my top five smarter marking ideas:

1 Use 'What? Why? How?' in all you teach and in all student response.
2 At the end of a piece of work, teachers often leave a comment. Keep this comment diagnostic; with a specific target for improvement. Consider a shorthand code in order to reduce rewriting the same opening statements over and over again. For example: WWH (What? Why? How?); IO (Improvements Only); TAG (Targets And Goals); EBI (Even Better If).
3 Outstanding feedback includes diagnostic comments with students responding to written feedback alongside the teacher's comments. Perhaps a reflection on their work or a comment on the assessment itself.
4 Embed routines where student A expects their work to be shared with student B and that student B will record their feedback for student A.
5 Ask students to redraft work two or three times, with a clear intention that the marking will become less and less prominent on the work each time is it modified.

Literateness

"I do not claim to be a literacy teacher, but I have a responsibility to be a teacher of literacy."

Focus on one keyword every lesson (remember quality, not quantity) and look into the definitions, pronunciations, related forms and historical origins of the word. You could even hunt out some memorable quotes from famous figures. Aim to impart this level of detailed information to your students at least once a lesson.

I have seen in many observations the teaching of five, sometimes even ten keywords that just get lost during the dynamics of the lesson. I am no literacy teacher, but I do know that my role as a classroom teacher comes with a responsibility to ensure words are spelt, pronounced and defined correctly. Below are my simple top tips for #Literateness.

1 Choose one keyword and break it down. A piece of vocabulary for GCSE or A-level students can easily be given to Year 7 or 8 students. For example, 'anthropometrics': break the word into parts such as 'anthro-' and 'metrics' and redefine these parts.

2 Dedicate a place in your classroom for project keywords. Ensure all students build up their own word bank at the back of their books.

3 Dedicate one part of your whiteboard and one part of *every* lesson for listing and teaching keywords.

4 Ask students to return to class having learnt the pronunciation and definition of a keyword for their project.

5 Make sure you have a dictionary in your classroom. Read it yourself. Choose a letter each lesson and a word to share and define.

Teaching tip

Be sure to share any new words that you learn yourself. Did you have to look something up while reading the newspaper? Do you know the words perfervid, exiguous, ephemeral? Look them up! Tweet a photo of a keyword that you have used in the classroom that is polished and well-understood by your students, using #Literateness. Only the complicated words of course!

Taking it further

Link learning and keywords to extension activities. Ask your class to write a poem or a short story using the day's keyword.

#Literateness

Numeral notions

"If people do not believe that mathematics is simple, it is only because they do not realise how complicated life is."
John von Neumann

We often find it tough to integrate Maths into other subject areas. Read on to discover some useful tricks.

Most non-Maths teachers I know struggle to link numeracy into lesson plans and their own subject teaching. Just as the focus for literacy is ever prevalent, numeracy will not go away. As the review of the curriculum and teacher standards are revised, the focus on numeracy is even clearer.

Start each lesson off, as you would with a keyword, by including a mathematical reference linked to the learning. For example, if students are studying the Battle of Hastings in 1066, ask them to work out how many years ago the battle was from today's date.

Other ideas include:

- Promote the importance of calculations in your classroom. Ensure all students build up their own references at the back of their books. For example, recording measurements, weight, timings, dates and periods of time.
- Dedicate one part of your whiteboard and one part of *every* lesson for calculating and teaching numeracy.
- Ask students to return to class having evidence of numeracy references for their project.
- Make sure you have a calculator in your classroom. Encourage simple calculator skills when measuring, calculating and generating graphs, shapes or fractions.

Bonus idea ★

Create a hopscotch calculator on the floor of your classroom. Use chalk or masking tape to construct the diagram and then encourage students to hop, skip or jump their way around key numbers. Have fun!

#YouDoTheMaths

Don't forget the gherkin

"Why put the gherkin in the burger when no one likes them?"

The 'burger lesson' involves a top, middle and bottom. This might be controversial, but I also love a gherkin in my burger; add a gherkin to your burger lesson planning today to give it that extra zing!

I love it when you devour a burger and your fangs bite down into the delights of a pickled gherkin! Similarly, the gherkin is the tipping point in your teaching; that eureka moment that happens once in a blue moon. The gherkin for me is that zesty taste in your mouth that makes you shiver all over, the moment you know your planning or your lesson is going to be outstanding! For example: the juncture in a child's learning when they suddenly grasp something, or the instant the hairs stand up on the back of your neck and you remember the real reason why you came into teaching.

Without the gherkin, that 'X factor' of teaching can often be lost. Conducting a very informal survey, Twitter teachers across the UK listed the following as the most vital aspects of lesson planning:

- Knowing the students sitting in front of you. Every name, all the data and their life story.
- #Stickability. What needs to stick? See Idea 87.
- Resilience. Real life context and reference.
- A pen and the five minute lesson plan, see Idea 9.

Ensure you consider these elements when planning all your lessons so that every one has a gherkin moment!

Taking it further

Buy a batch of paper plates and ask the students to organise the next lesson by dividing the time up and writing down what should happen next. Make sure you highlight the gherkin moment!

#Gherkin

Meet and greet, end and send

"One foot in the classroom, one foot in the corridor."

'Meet and greet, end and send' is a simple strategy for doorstep motivation into and out of your classroom.

Teaching tip

Create a simple memory sign to place in your teacher planner. Download a template online at: www.bloomsbury.com/TeacherToolkit

Try sitting at your teacher's desk for the start and end of a lesson and compare this against the same class when you stand at your classroom door (with one foot in the classroom and one foot in the corridor) for the start and end of another lesson. How does the atmosphere vary? Is there a clear difference from how both lessons start and end? I'm sure there is!

Repeating this process and making it your routine can reinforce the importance of ensuring a calm entrance and exit to each lesson. The positive repercussion for the whole school is that every teacher will be present on the corridor at the start and end of every lesson, ensuring high standards of behaviour, punctuality and teaching and learning. It's also good exercise to regularly get up out of your chair! Come up with ideas for 4 detailed 'meet and greet' routines; below are some 'end and send' ones:

- End on time – One foot in the classroom, one foot in the corridor.
- Wave goodbye – Say 'see you next lesson!'
- Provide any prompts as students exit. Ensure a calm dismissal.

Share your start and end ethos with students and make this a classroom routine.

Don't drink and teach!

"I'm old-fashioned and I was trained under the guise of intensive and soldierly practice."

Just put that cup of tea down for a moment and give your students 100%!

I know this idea may stir controversy and perhaps go down like a ton of feathers, but give it some thought the next time you see a mug of tea in a classroom. I'm not advocating dehydration in return for teaching outstanding lessons; I'm just posing a question of professionalism versus practicality.

Why drinking tea in a lesson doesn't work:

- If you're drinking a cup of tea during a lesson are you really giving your class your full attention? Teaching without due care and attention is unprofessional.
- Professional standards. Would you accept students drinking hot chocolate in your lesson?
- What about accidents? What if your mug falls over and burns you or the students? What if your beverage damages the internal workings of a keyboard? Stains a textbook or a student's exercise book?
- What if you were being observed? We should always treat every lesson as if we are being observed. Have you ever watched someone teach a class with one hand holding a mug? It looks awful!

> **Teaching tip**
>
> Call me old-fashioned but you won't find a kettle in my classroom! Drinking tea is limited to break times and lunchtime. Limit yourself to just keeping a bottle of water in the classroom, and remember, hydration leads to outstanding learning.

#TeaTeaching

The 7ePlan

"Making knowledge meaningful in our own minds."

Use the 7ePlan to plan more effectively. It is based on the seven stages in the learning cycle, which are: elicit, engage, explore, explain, elaborate, evaluate and extend.

I first began designing the 7ePlan after reading about constructivism, the 7e learning model (Lawson, 1995 narrated by Kanlı, 2007) and also coming across @TeacherToolkit's 5MinPlan on Twitter. As a lead practitioner, I am constantly looking for ways to help teachers plan more effectively. The 7ePlan is a simple planning template that can be used to quickly plan a lesson sequence. It also incorporates all the key features that are needed to gain an outstanding judgment in your formal lesson observations.

The constructivist approach, on which the 7e structure is based, is a learning process that helps learners to make their knowledge meaningful in their own mind (Fardanesh, 2006). This approach is focused on learning environments, which give individuals a chance to construct knowledge by themselves, or by discussing with other individuals. In learning by exploring, students construct their new knowledge by basing the knowledge around their environments (Saab et al., 2005).

The 7e learning model is an approach that considers how learning happens to better sequence learning activities or episodes. According to the 7e learning model, each person comes to the learning environment with their own prior knowledge and they construct their new learning based on this knowledge.

1 **Elicit**: what do students already know? Some fun ways to gauge existing knowledge include quick quizzes, Post-it notes, mini whiteboards, traffic lights etc. This is also a good opportunity to deal with any misunderstandings.

2 **Engage**: why is this lesson interesting? In this stage you want to engage interest and curiosity, raise the big questions.

3 **Explore**: what can students find out? Students should be given opportunities to work together, independent of you, the teacher.

4 **Explain**: what input is needed from the teacher to formalise the concept? Encourage your students to explain concepts and definitions in their own words, ask for justification and clarification before providing them with new labels, definitions and theory.

5 **Elaborate**: how can students apply and demonstrate their learning?

6 **Extend**: how can you encourage students to apply or extend the concept in a new situation? Students make connections not just in the subject/ideas studied but also beyond it. They are able to apply ideas/generalise and transfer principles.

7 **Evaluate**: how much progress have students made? Evaluation should include self-reflection from the student.

by @HThompson1982

Bonus idea ★

Take a look at an outstanding example of the 7e plan in use online at: www.bloomsbury.com/TeacherToolkit. Join in the conversation on Twitter, share your experiences of using the 7e plan using the hashtag #7ePlan!

#7ePlan

The bell is for me, not for you

"Timing is everything."

Break your lesson down into a simple pattern for lesson planning. Use five minutes for the starter activity and setting context; take 15 minutes for teacher talk, a plenary task and for questioning, spread out throughout the lesson; and use 35 minutes for the main student activity. Leave five minutes at the end for packing away.

Have you ever found yourself, or heard a colleague saying: 'The bell is for me, not for you.' What was the context for this? Timing? Punctuality? Behaviour? I'm confident that the statement does not derive from positive behaviour management or astute lesson planning. Timing is everything when it comes to outstanding teaching. Here are some above-the-parapet suggestions for sharp lesson control.

1 Put one clock on the wall facing you and another clock on the wall facing the students. Make sure your own clock is five minutes faster, thus ensuring a prompt end to the lesson, with at least five minutes for a plenary.

2 Download Triptico or another clock counter for your classroom computer. Having a clock counter on display with a 'tick tock' sound oozing out of the whiteboard speakers ensures pace.

3 Always inform students of the time provided to complete the activity. Provide clear timing reminders and adjust them if necessary. If you know your students well, then you've probably planned the timings to a nanosecond.

4 Use an egg timer to time parts of the lesson, particularly when you are talking.

5 If you cannot finish your lesson before the bell rings then there is something not quite right. If you can't teach it all in the allotted time, cut it out!

> **Bonus idea** ★
>
> We have just removed the bell in my current school. This ensures teachers are always keeping a closer eye on the time and finishing lessons promptly. Why not suggest this at your school?

The 3Gs

"Outstanding = A systematic and consistently applied approach to behaviour management."

For good, quick lesson planning which will build on good behaviour management, use the 3Gs.

When all 3Gs are placed together they create a modest formula for Outstanding teaching: Good planning = Good teaching = Good learning. It's that simple! We can see in this formula that planning is of paramount importance in order to move students towards good engagement and behaviour.

Now, let us explore the concept of 'Flipped Learning', which originated in the USA. In 1990, Professor Mazur of Harvard University found that 'computer-aided instruction allowed him to coach instead of lecture'. The idea stemmed from peer instruction, which involves 'moving information *transfer* out and moving information *assimilation* into the classroom'.

Twenty years later, we are fully hooked into the digital age, where flipped learning is far more common practice than we realise. Coursework, examinations, homework and teaching can all be completed online before, during or after the actual allocated teaching session.

So, let's flip the 3Gs model in the same way flipped learning encourages teachers and students to assimilate information from outside, into the classroom.

Good teaching = good learning = and *informs* good planning.

Or

Good learning = *informs* good planning = and *develops* good teaching.

Teaching tip

Either approach to this simplified model encourages planning or learning to inform better teaching. And that's what it's all about isn't it? Better teaching. Why not give it a go? Use the learning to inform your next lesson plan, ask your students to plan their own lesson!

Assessment

Part 3

Crossing the curricular

"Excellent subject knowledge with cross-curricular references sets out the benchmark for outstanding teaching and learning."

Make a habit of linking day to day situations at home and at school, in your lesson planning, with subjects across the school, so that students can make references to knowledge, skills and understanding in other subjects.

When talking with your colleagues always ask about what they are doing in their classroom. If you teach Year 8 Art, find out what your students are studying in Science and look for opportunities to link the two curricula. Curricular links such as sketching organisms, cell functions and reproductive patterns would be ideal.

Low planning impact:

- Probe deeper into student discussions to examine cross-curricular thinking.
- Keep a daily newspaper on your desk.
- Build up a collection of textbooks from other subjects.

Medium planning impact:

- Create a classroom wall display to provide a wall of images as sources of evidence. This could include iconic newspaper images, magazine front covers, branding and even the school ethos.
- Display a large world map. This is probably the simplest and easiest way to reference the location of current affairs.

High planning impact:

- Collate resources from other subjects to use in your own lesson planning.
- Provide subject references week by week in a carefully planned scheme of work.

> **Teaching tip**
>
> Plan for a student presentation day of two subjects with both teachers assessing student references to both subjects.

> **Bonus idea** ★
>
> Create a series of homework tasks that specifically ask students to return their independent contributions using references to a planned sequence of subjects. For example week one = Maths; week two = English; week three = Science.

The five minute marking plan (part 1)

"Speed up your marking!"

First things first, identify your success criteria at the planning stage.

The concept of Key Marking Points (KMPs) sits right in the middle of the five minute marking plan. It is central to teacher and student clarity, aids engagement and gives self-direction to a student's efforts. The KMPs describe how both the teacher and the students know that they have been successful.

Get students to devise their own KMPs for a task by giving them spoof pieces of work (anonymised work produced by another class or the previous year) at different grades or levels. Which piece of work is better? Can you say why? Once a teacher and the students know 'What A Good One Looks Like' (WAGOLL) they can start to work towards an excellent piece of work or performance. Marking can be a rather long and unexciting task, but once you have a clear framework for marking:

- The task of marking speeds up.
- Feedback becomes far more informative as it can be linked to Key Marking Points. Why not number the Key Marking Points and give feedback by simply writing the appropriate number at the bottom of a student's work as either 'what went well' or 'even better if'.
- Students can both self and peer-assess their work, including each other's before they hand it in for you to mark.

by @LeadingLearner

Teaching tip

Use the Key Marking Points to identify common errors made by students and build in time to reteach things they have not understood properly.

Taking it further

You can download the template online at: www.bloomsbury.com/ TeacherToolkit and read more details at: www.bit. ly/More5MinMarkingPlan.

#5MinMarkingPlan

Covert press-ganging

"Opportunities for redrafting = smart outcomes."

Detailed oral and written feedback should be provided so learners know how well they have done and how to improve. This is no easy feat in every lesson, so read on for a few covert ideas to ensure all students are reading, responding to and acting on feedback without even knowing it.

The simplest idea for teachers embedding redrafting as a learning process is to name all pieces of work as a draft! In my own subject Design Technology, this is naturally placed in the design process for developing ideas through a sequence of initial ideas, developed ideas and a final idea. This process is spoiled by the teaching technique of asking students to complete five ideas in order to move forward!

So, here are my top five covert press-ganging opportunities to encourage students to love drafting and redrafting work time and time again, not for the purpose of delaying or jumping through hoops, but for the process of learning and acting on feedback.

1 Come up with your own simple colour coded tracking system that monitors a sequence of classwork. The tracker will flag up that Billy Cheater has moved onto stage two without completing the first part of the process, therefore missing a vital opportunity for initial feedback in order to ensure progress and impact at an earlier stage.

Kaine Alwaysfirst
• Stage One: Rough Ideas – completed
• Stage Two: Redrafting Rough Ideas – in process

Ahmed Cutscorners
• Stage One: Rough Ideas – in process – falling behind

Billy Cheater
- Stage One: Rough Ideas – incomplete
- Stage Two: Redrafting Rough Ideas – in process

Nafisa Do-Good
- Stage One: Rough Ideas – completed
- Stage Two: Redrafting Rough Ideas – completed
- Stage Three: Final Ideas – in process.

2 Introduce a keyword and ask your students to highlight a sentence in their work. Students are then asked to redraft the same sentence using the keyword and alternative vocabulary.

3 Ask students to swap their work and get each student to take responsibility for editing, adding to or cutting their work based on what they have learnt.

4 In small groups get your students to take turns to scrutinise and improve each other's work, before presenting what they have modified to the other groups.

5 Set a 100 words challenge, then redraft to 75 words, and then 50 words. The challenge is for students to keep all the main points and to self-correct.

Taking it further

Consider verbal feedback strategies too; not everything needs to be written down. Make it habitual; that student responses are rephrased with additional keywords connected to demonstrate assimilated progress.

Bonus idea ★

Create two or three press reporters who will be equipped with a series of teacher questions aimed at investigating and probing other students in the class. Each reporter should be given an objective to achieve and perhaps do this in secret. Who can provide the greatest difference in first to second redrafted pieces of work? Which student demonstrates a full understanding of today's keyword?

#CovertFeedback

Assertive acolytes

"The definition of an acolyte is someone who performs ceremonial duties. The Greek and Latin origins of the work mean attendant."

Encourage your students to be confident, self-respecting individuals using the assertive acolytes technique.

'Confident Learners' is a term taken from the Curriculum for Excellence in Scotland. The concept encourages students to develop self-respect, a sense of wellbeing, with secure values and beliefs, whilst the ambitious attribute emerges. For me, this is about encouraging students to become assertive acolytes (see Teaching tip for definition).

Here are my top ten strategies for developing assertive acolytes in your classroom:

1 Create a climate for all students to express their feelings, thoughts and desires.
2 Establish a set time in each lesson or project where all students are expected to take part.
3 Make sure all students understand the necessity for routine and duty.
4 Create a simple list of expectations when debating values and beliefs.
5 Encourage positive thinking, commentary and feedback. Define what success is.
6 Provide an opportunity for ambition and success to be celebrated and rewarded.
7 Showcase the difference between non-assertiveness and assertiveness.
8 Place a large mirror on the wall and inspire students to present ideas to themselves.
9 Make sure no one is left behind. Discuss failure and encourage risk.
10 Most importantly, students must manage themselves to grow into confident assertive acolytes.

Dangerous taxation

"Dangerous: able to cause harm and likely to cause problems, or to have adverse consequences."

Use toy money to teach your students the concept of taxation and financial intelligence.

The levy of tax affects us all and hits our pay cheques hard! This idea uses the usual credit and debit system commonly found in schools to reward good grades and good behaviour but also uses the concept of tax. Discuss with your class the variety of ways you can pay for education. If achieving qualifications equated to money, what would an A* be worth or a D? Of course, this is just a bit of fun, it's not all about grades, but it is an interesting experiment! How can you introduce dangerous taxation?

1 Grab an old board game that uses toy money, you might need to photocopy the notes to have enough for the whole class.
2 Distribute the cash equally amongst your students and explain the tariffs.
3 Reward students with a ten pound note each time they achieve something great. Or if you want to link this idea to assessment then reward each time a student moves up one sub-level, i.e. level 4.0 to a 4.3.
4 Link the tax charges to your assessment criteria. For example, if students do not complete the lesson objective, they receive a fine and you take away some fake cash.

The sight of pretend money will get your students excited and motivated to complete work and see their mock bank accounts rise and fall with glee.

Teaching tip

Try setting up the bank for a week to see how it goes. If it's a disaster you can always share the lessons of bankruptcy!

Taking it further

Offer incentives for completing extended lesson objectives such as homework or going the extra mile.

#CashForGrades

#Bananas

"Banana fact: you can use the inside of a banana peel to clean and polish leather shoes."

Consider using marking to inform lesson planning.

Hands up: who loves marking? Err, ok. I'll move on... Assessment does not purely have to be formative or summative. Consider banana assessment! Write down all the banana adjectives you can think of: yellow; potassium; energy; slip; skin; mad; deranged; bemused; crazy; daft and so on. We should consider our classroom teacher assessments in this way; there are many variants that can all lead to a form of madness if not too careful! We can become bombarded with the constant slog to assess, tick-and-flick, stamp, add a sticker, provide a comment, give constructive feedback, red pen, green pen and whatever else we can think of!

Marking on the whole is a waste of time. Why? Well, as my good friend @MrLockyer claims, 'marking is broken!' and it rarely benefits the teacher or the student. Stephen Lockyer suggests that it can be fixed. Here's how: we simply need to look at the way we mark. Who are the marking stakeholders?

- the students;
- the Ofsted inspectors;
- the headteacher;
- the parents and
- the teachers.

But who are the key participants? The student and the teacher. How can you maximise opportunities for both? Stephen Lockyer says, 'marking is planning'. Use marking to inform your planning, rather than see a lesson or a test as an outcome to produce marking.

Taking it further

Consider immediate feedback. One-to-one, marking work with them, even if it's just for 30 seconds. Students will appreciate the immediate response and personal attention.

#Bananas

Bloom's Post-it

"We once covered a student from head to toe in Post-it notes!"

Carry a set of colour coded sticky Post-it notes in your teacher's pencil case.

Use Post-it notes when you address the objectives of Bloom's taxonomy. They are especially useful for peer-to-peer assessment and when students are assessing their own work. Using this method, based on the various colours that represent each stage of the higher order questioning framework, has supported students in understanding the meaning of 'continuous development'. This is a crucial activity to challenge students to progress within their area of study.

- Pink Post-it: Students must provide an explanation of the definition.
- Orange Post-it: Students must provide a detailed example of the explanation.
- Yellow Post-it: Students need to describe the advantages of the example provided.
- Green Post-it: Students need to describe the disadvantages of the example provided.

Look at the grading criteria of the work and ask students to identify what their current grade is, they then must identify what their target grade is. Students then peer assess their work by using the 'arrow-shaped' Post-it notes to check their work.

by @MoheeniPatel

Taking it further

As a starter activity, you could display a piece of unfinished work on your interactive whiteboard so students can use different coloured Post-it notes to write comments on it.

Bonus idea ★

Students love self-assessment and peer-to-peer assessment. If possible, encourage students to use their mobile phone, by taking a picture of the interactive whiteboard with everyone's sticky notes stuck on the board. This is a great way to reflect back on the work at a later date.

#PostIt

#SOLO

"What the hell is SOLO?"

When probing for the purpose of the learning or when self-assessing learning outcomes, ask students for 'thumbs up' or 'thumbs down'.

SOLO is useful for ensuring student-led learning increases complexity in their understanding. The SOLO taxonomy was developed by Biggs and Collis, 1982 and stands for: **S**tructure of **O**bserved **L**earning **O**utcomes. SOLO categorises a student's understanding by assessing the cumulative complexity of their work against five stages. Equally, there are links with Bloom's Taxonomy in the cognitive domain. The representation here, as in Bloom's, is the assumption that each level embraces previous levels, but adds something more:

1 **Pre-structural**: a student has no prior knowledge and is simply obtaining isolated information, which has no organisation and makes no logical sense.
2 **Unistructural**: a student may know something and noticeable connections are made, but the full meaning is not comprehended.
3 **Multistructural**: a student can show a number of connections but cannot connect their significance for the whole.
4 **Relational**: a student is now able to appreciate several significant parts in relation to the whole and can make connections between them.
5 At the **extended abstract level** a student can make connections within new contexts and new subject areas to transfer the principles to other areas of their learning.

Taking it further

Why not share SOLO with your senior leadership team? SOLO can be expended not only in assessment, but also in designing the curriculum in terms of the learning outcomes intended. Consider reading his website: www.bit.ly/BiggsAndSOLO.

Bonus idea ★

Here is a great video on YouTube, explaining how SOLO works using Lego. www.bit.ly/SOLOTaxonomy.

 #SOLO

A good going over!

"Outstanding = prior learning is assessed systematically and accurately."

Make sure that learning is boosted in your classroom by assessing and sharing success criteria with your students.

Early on in my career I was sometimes hesitant to test students. I dreaded the marking it generated and found myself testing less and less. However, I soon came to comprehend the power of giving students 'a good going over' and the importance of assessing learning and providing feedback. Students are hungry to know how they are doing. It is our duty to keep them well informed. Cast your mind back to when you were at school. Ask yourself the following questions about how you were learning:

Teaching tip

Try using Idea 20, the five minute marking plan, to focus on what should or should not be assessed.

- Were you aware of your baseline starting point for assessment?
- Did testing provide you with the opportunity to boost your learning?
- How often were you informed about the progress you were making?
- Did intervention exist? As a result of an assessment, did something happen for you? Did you suddenly move groups as a result?
- Did your assessments offer any enrichment opportunities, such as going on a field trip?

How to combat large piles of marking:

- Display work around the classroom with banners indicating levels/grades.
- Share the success criteria every lesson.
- Provide scaffolding templates and writing frames.
- Encourage students to mark their work through peer and self-assessment.
- Ensure departmental time regularly includes marking and moderation opportunities.

Taking it further

Ask your students to curate their own self-assessment task for their forthcoming assessment. Give them a selection of options – offer choice and increasing levels of difficulty – so that they feel part of the process.

The five minute marking plan (part 2)

"The two-way street of feedback."

Feedback isn't just for students. Learn about which parts of your teaching programme have been successful and which need revising by evaluating your marking and asking your students.

The effective promotion of assessment for learning requires teachers to recognise that feedback is a two-way process. Teachers must also find ways of receiving better feedback from learners.

Evaluative marking is often the forgotten part of marking and assessment. Marking can be used to help give feedback to teachers about which parts of the teaching programme has worked well and what needs to be rethought. This is often called evaluative assessment or marking and is a very useful way of continually improving the quality of schemes of work and lesson plans.

As well as the feedback from marking, it is very easy to get feedback from students and then add your own reflective thoughts into the mix. What would you say if when reflecting on the last topic you taught and you were asked, 'what are you unhappy about with the teaching of that topic?' What would your students say if you asked them the same question? This is all part of being a reflective professional.

You can download the template online at: www.bloomsbury.com/TeacherToolkit and read more details at: www.bit.ly/More5MinMarkingPlan.

by @LeadingLearner

F.A.I.L.

"First Attempt In Learning!"

Draft, redraft and redraft again. Ensure your students know that a first attempt at a piece of work just isn't going to cut it in your classroom.

At a conference recently, Professor Barry Hymer, from the University of Cumbria, shared this fantastic analogy. He was visiting a school and kept seeing the letters F.A.I.L. emblazoned all over the walls. When he asked a student what it meant, they said: 'First Attempt In Learning'. Consider what a remarkable feat it is to successfully shift students' mindset in this way. A word like 'fail' is so emotive, especially in the school environment, but this simple acronym gives students the encouragement and confidence to be able to receive and accept constructive criticism to improve their work. Be prepared to send students' homework back home for redrafting!

- When pieces of work are submitted, invite the class to provide their feedback.
- Remind students to be constructive. They should be 'hard on content but soft on people'.
- Feedback should be specific and helpful.
- After the feedback is given from peers, students are invited to redraft their work.
- Be sure to highlight the improvement and progress between drafts. It is important that students can record evidence of the work they are completing.

So, why not give this idea a try? Embed in your classroom that all homework will be a F.A.I.L.

Taking it further

For a further discussion on the benefits of redrafting work, read this fabulous blog post by David Didau: 'Improving peer-feedback with public critique'. www.bit.ly/DavidDidau. Also watch the video at www.bit.ly/AustinsButterfly

Teaching

Part 4

Use me, I'm a TA!

"How often have you wished you had an extra pair of hands or an extra few hours in the day?"

Teaching Assistants (TAs) should be involved in lesson planning and good communication should always be evident between teacher and TA. Speak with them now!

A TA is someone who supports a teacher in the classroom. Having one in your lesson is a valuable commodity, but evidence from the Education Endowment Foundation suggests that the impact TAs have on learning in the classroom is far from effective, with a 'very low or no impact in return for high cost'. The TA's duties can differ dramatically from school to school. But students will always need additional educational needs support and the emphasis should always remain on supporting students and that alone. Use your TA effectively by:

- Involving them in lesson planning and schemes of work.
- Making them welcome in your classroom and directing them regularly.
- Providing a lesson plan with differentiated activities for students that need support.
- Providing the differentiated resources and facilitating proceedings.
- Beyond one-to-one support, allocating additional groups of children who need extra support.
- Offering additional literacy or numeracy tasks. If your TA is a linguist, ask them to translate key resources. Involve your TA in question and answer discussions with students. Direct them to support small groups of students for literacy and numeracy intervention as part of your lesson planning.

I'm different!

"Sir, I learn best by doing it this way!"

Provide students with a modest choice of activities; or subtly, a directed choice. This will ensure students can engage with classwork and be challenged at the right level. This can be as simple as referencing levels or eliminating certain elements for specific students.

Outstanding teaching requires a deep level of planned differentiation and pitch. This doesn't have to be difficult, but no matter what you do, plan differentiation 'by input'.

1 Provide some students with a worksheet (perhaps a writing frame) and others with none.
2 Offer a choice of resources/activities that vary in difficulty and encourage students to make at least two choices, including one resource/activity that they MUST complete. Having a choice will reduce embarrassment but also encourage students to be selective and set their own challenge.
3 Appoint two or three student leaders, or one per table or group, to lead the learning of others. The best examples I have seen not only include gifted and talented students, but students who speak second or third languages who can help students translate learning into English.
4 Invite students to lead a starter activity or a PE lesson warm-up.
5 Challenge students who have struggled to teach others what they have learnt and assess this by observing the outcome. This is also a perfect strategy to deploy for students who arrive late or have been absent.

Teaching tip

Consider a quick and 95% accurate do-it-yourself translation of classroom worksheets, by copying and pasting the content into a popular search engine translation service.

Taking it further

Reach an outstanding level of lesson planning by trying out my differentiated questioning template; available to download and modify online at: www.bloomsbury.com/TeacherToolkit

Beyond AfL

"Just by seating my top four students at each corner of the room I noticed an improvement in the performance of the whole class!"

Follow Eric Mazur's lead and try thinking outside the box when it comes to seating arrangements, homework setting and lesson planning.

Teaching tip

Why not switch your seating plan around every half-term to see how different combinations work? I rotate my student positions– without fail – every half-term. Consider high-ability students sitting in each corner.

I do not need to introduce you to Assessment for Learning (AfL), so I won't. What I'd like to do is give you something more to think about. How can you take AfL further? More explicitly, how can you take AfL beyond the classroom?

Peer Instruction (PI) is an evidence-based, interactive teaching method developed by Harvard Professor Eric Mazur in the early 1990s at Harvard University. It's a student-centred approach that involves flipping the traditional system by moving learning out of the classroom. To you and me, this is called homework!

Mazur also proposed another method called Just in Time Teaching (JiTT). Before a lesson, students do preparation work such as pre-lesson reading and answering questions. This allows the lesson time to be used more efficiently; the teacher is free to engage students with more in-depth questioning and is able to carry out assessment that is more tailored to student abilities. To you and me, this is called planned homework and lesson planning!

This is nothing new for us today, but it probably would have been pretty ground breaking in the 1990s. I have great respect for Mazur to have formalised something concrete like this, progressing the thought of the time. Other PI ideas from Mazur include seating arrangements. He discovered that when lower ability students are seated at the front, their learning increases. Meanwhile, the results of high ability students who are seated in the back are not affected. In addition, Mazur's research indicates that when high performing students are seated in the outer four corners of the classroom, the performance of the class as a whole increases.

Mazur's questioning procedure:

1 The instructor poses questions based on students' responses to their pre-class reading.
2 Students reflect on the questions.
3 Students respond with answers.
4 The teacher reviews student responses.
5 Students discuss their thinking and answers with their peers.
6 Students then commit again to an individual answer.
7 The teacher again reviews responses and decides whether more explanation is needed before moving on to the next concept.

Taking it further

Read more about Mazur's research at: www.bit.ly/EMazurPeer and www.bit.ly/EMazur. Mazur discusses how "JiTT works asynchronously out of class, and PI gives real-time feedback" and how combining these approaches is beneficial for improving learning and skill development.

#BAfL

Game, set and match!

"Outstanding = Tasks are challenging, and match students needs accurately."

Just like tennis, 'game, set and match' can be applied to the classroom. Consider your teaching to be a sequence of episodes for learning that lead students into achieving one outcome, several outcomes or everything you had planned!

Try using the tennis scoring system to split projects of work into games, sets and matches, perhaps even championships and Grand Slams! The method will clearly show students' progression and differentiate.

Game: is the lesson planning itself, but it is far from a game. Consider your teaching of one lesson in a scheme of work as an element to the bigger picture. Every lesson counts. It is important that students have the opportunity to win. Match up your resources for the lesson to each individual student.

Set: is a sequence of lessons that form part of a topic. Consider providing students with a set of resources that they can bank or exchange with other students of varying abilities.

Match: is the actual culmination of lessons that enable students to complete a project. If the game and set are carefully pitched, there is no reason why you cannot provide every single student with an array of resources that they can use to build upon throughout acquisition of knowledge.

Pitch perfect

"The teaching is exactly right in tone."

Display a bar chart or a graph and create a huge arrow with a message emblazoned across it saying 'This lesson is pitched here.'

Pitch, in a musical sense, is the degree of height or depth of a tone or sound. The sound produced can sometimes go wrong, it can be flat or sharp. This is quite often the case in teaching too. We can get it wrong and pitch the learning too low (the lesson is boring) or too high (it becomes frustrating). Think about the following points when planning your lessons to become pitch perfect.

Pitch perfect planning:

1 Do you have access to the latest classroom data?
2 Do you have access to all student support plans, statements and reports?
3 What information will you use for this lesson? Which information will you ignore?
4 What are the success criteria for high and low ability students?
5 What is Plan B if Plan A fails? Which parts of each plan are imaginative?

Analysis of pitch:

1 Were all the students engaged? Were there any low-level behavioural events?
2 Did all your students complete the work set?
3 Did troublesome Michelle Know-It-All remain engaged and make progress? Was it 'rapid progress'?
4 How did you monitor the extension activities set for Nafisa Stops-When-I'm-Not-Looking?
5 Which techniques worked well? What else could you do if you had more time?

Taking it further

Encourage students to vote for the lesson's degree of difficulty. This could be adapted in light of cold winters and hot summer afternoons. Of course, your planning and subject knowledge will ensure that nothing is lost and you simply call their bluff!

Bonus idea

Display three versions of class activity and spin the arrow to select what version is taught!

#PitchPerfect

What? Me?!

"Outstanding lessons demand that expectations are consistently high."

Rather than shouting, walk over and sit down next to the student and speak on their level.

#WhatMe

Does this sound familiar? You call out Bryan Swagger-By-Style's name. He jolts upright, looks at you baffled; he turns his head to a friend and then looks back at you, lifting his palms to the air and raising his arms aloft, he exclaims 'What? Me?! It wasn't me!' Now, I'm sure we've all seen this in action in our classrooms when our expectations are so high that even the best of our students can be caught off-guard in the most testing situations.

Delivering high-pitched, dour or didactic lessons can leave students yearning for freedom. These lessons cannot be avoided during coursework, revision and assessment periods, or when you are just not up for a jazz hands lesson and really need to just get your students to knuckle down.

'What? Me?!' stems from those of you who want to teach consistently outstanding lessons and grow frustrated with students who show that slightest ebb of focus in a lesson.

If you do encounter the 'What? Me?!' in you lesson, then here is what to do:

1 Share your expectations. Encourage your expectations to be pooled by the class.
2 Double check that these expectations are sensible, achievable and realistic.
3 Make the class own these expectations. Avoid the word 'rules' at all costs.

Be vigilant!

"If you popped in to observe your own child in a classroom, what would you hope to see?"

Make a list and carefully examine the relevance and effectiveness of your interventions.

Intervention relates to use of support in and out of the classroom. It might be deploying TAs effectively; using a range of differentiation strategies; or focusing on the use of literacy and numeracy to support learning. Whatever the case may be, your interventions have to be relevant and must enable progress. For example, how does the teaching of keywords enable all students to improve their learning? The 2012 Ofsted report reminds us that intervention and support must be 'appropriate and have notable impact'. An outstanding teacher must be vigilant to meet this challenge and ensure that they can provide evidence of learning and progress over time. How do you ensure your interventions have notable impact?

1 Do you consciously know what your interventions are and why they are needed?
2 Do you monitor, evaluate and review the resources that you provide? What impact do they make? When is the best time to review them?
3 Do you ask your students for their opinions about the interventions you provide? Do you ask your students' parents?
4 How much do you plan your interventions?
5 How do you decide who needs an intervention? How often do they happen?

Incite

"What did your parents really think about you as a child?"

Sharing your own achievements, difficulties, hopes and dreams can build and reinforce your relationships with your students and encourage and motivate them to achieve.

Every teacher has their own history and their own circumstances. 'Incite' is designed to foster relationships in the classroom. Relationships between students and teachers need to be cultivated in order to work through issues that might affect attendance, behaviour, attitudes to learning and ability.

Students are not interested in a show off; nor are they interested in your sob stories. But, as time gradually passes by and relationships flounder or grow, a natural opportunity will arise to offer students your words of wisdom. These may include some 'show off' stories, as well as those that would make us feel more grateful, or others that would have your class crying with laughter. Incite is your life story used to encourage and motivate your students. Consider sharing the following:

1 Describe your school behaviour.
2 Talk about a time when you let your parents down.
3 Consider sharing parts of a bereavement, an emergency or another major event.
4 Share your dreams. Even if you teach until you're 68, what will you do next?
5 Talk about a chore that you have found difficult, maybe paying the utility bills, finding a job, planning a family celebration.
6 Share a heart-to-heart about how you dealt with problems in your worst school subjects.

#Incite

Emotional roller coaster

"Breathe deeply, breathe slowly."

We all suffer from bereavements, illnesses, accidents and stress; we may be teachers, but we are still human. Emotional well-being in the classroom is all about balance. Remember emotional intelligence at all times.

A few headteachers may scorn at those who bring their own life circumstances into the classroom, but the finest headteachers I know will accept that even the best of us can wobble. It's how we overcome these situations, whilst remaining constantly secure in our own classroom practice, that is paramount to you and your students. So, imagine this scenario. Your headteacher's P.A has just frantically searched the school and has located you. They sit you down in a quiet office to deliver some devastating news. You are 15 minutes away from teaching Year 8 after break. How would you respond? How do you deal with the emotional roller coaster?

> **Teaching tip**
>
> Always have a box of tissues in your office and classroom. You never know when you (or someone else) might need it!

1 Consider your options. Teach or not to teach? If it's the latter, who needs to know and how can you tell them quickly?
2 If you do decide to teach, will you adapt your lesson plan? Will the change create additional stress?
3 If a student senses a mood change or thinks you are hot under the collar, how would you deal with this?
4 If your voice trembles when questioned, pause. Bite your lip. Squeeze two fingers together (hard)!
5 If all else fails, ask students to carry on with their work whilst you gather your thoughts.

So, what if?

"...you stopped teaching?"

Would the world end if you weren't there? Would your students be able to get on with their work? Take a small risk. Take a back seat in your classroom and ask your students what and how they would teach a topic if they were placed in your shoes.

It's the control freak inside all of us that rings the alarm bell at the thought of letting go and stepping back. The various demands, requirements, targets and standards we face can often hinder us taking risks in the classroom, but if we gradually get used to the idea, we can allow students to become more resilient and open up the floor to more student-led activities. How would you do this? How could you do this gradually so that it became the norm? To be truly resilient, students need to build up an aptitude to become robust, spirited and hardy so that they gradually become self-sufficient. So, what if you...

- rotated yourself around each of your student tables and worked with students in small groups?
- limited yourself to a small number of words or set amount of time to talk?
- asked students to take turns to lead parts of the lesson each week?
- asked for a teaching assistant to co-lead?
- asked the students to teach you something during the lesson?

Taking it further

Nominate a student to be the teacher. They will have the freedom to speak, question, answer and explain all conversations in the classroom. Rotate the role.

#WhatIfTeacher

Behaviour

Part 5

Sweat the small stuff

"Outstanding = Students' attitudes to learning are exemplary."

Prioritise consistency in your lessons to ensure low-level behaviour is not tolerated.

Developing attitudes to learning so that exemplary behaviour is evident, day-in-day-out, is no easy task. Don't kid yourself for a moment that it is. Textbook behaviour takes years of practise. So, how do we avoid poor behaviour creeping into our lessons, especially in those lessons when we're feeling a little below par, or the lessons that we've not planned as thoroughly as we might have. How do we ensure that standards do not falter? The answer? Consistency.

To ensure that all students learn and thrive in an atmosphere of respect and dignity relies on consistency across the whole school. But, I argue, that this can be achieved in your own domain, no matter how poor systems are across the school, or what kind of day you are having.

- ALWAYS ensure your lesson has an element of learning to capture very high levels of engagement.
- ALWAYS promote courtesy and be polite.
- ALWAYS uphold collaboration and cooperation no matter what. Stamp on those who hamper peer-to-peer learning.
- ALWAYS follow a systematic, consistently applied approach to behaviour management.
- NEVER allow a lesson to proceed with any kind of interruption. Nip low-level poor behaviour in the bud!

You will have to fight a few battles. As a good friend once said to me, 'you will need to sweat the small stuff'.

#SsS

The golden rule

"Do unto others what you would have them do unto you."

Teaching is full of golden rules, but the original one gives us a lesson in mutual respect, tolerance and equality.

The same concept has appeared to us in many different guises throughout history and across religions, each time advocating respect for others. The rule is a valuable reminder that respect should be a foundation stone of all teacher/student relationships.

Take a look at the different iterations of the rule from across the ages:

- Christianity: "Therefore all things whatsoever would that men should do to you, do ye even so to them." (Matthew 7:12)
- Confucius: "What you do not wish for yourself, do not do to others."
- Islam: "None of you [truly] believes until he wishes for his brother what he wishes for himself." (An-Nawawi's Forty Hadith 13, pg. 56)
- Judaism: "You shall not take vengeance or bear a grudge against your kinsfolk. Love your neighbor as yourself." (Leviticus 19:18)
- Sikhism: "I am a stranger to no one, and no one is a stranger to me. Indeed, I am a friend to all." (Guru Granth Sahib pg. 1299)
- Taoism: "The sage has no interest of his own, but takes the interests of the people as his own. He is kind to the kind; he is also kind to the unkind: for Virtue is kind." (Tao Teh Ching, Chapter 49)
- Hinduism: "One should never do that to another which one regards as injurious to one's own self." Brihaspati, Mahabharata (Anusasana Parva, Section CXIII, Verse 8)

Taking it further

Discuss these quotes in a classroom debate. Try tackling fundamental values including democracy, the rule of law, individual liberty and tolerance of those with different faiths and beliefs. What are your students' thoughts on these concepts? What do they know about ethics and traditions in other cultures?

Smiley faces

"The simplest behaviour model in the world!"

If you move around and work in different classrooms, or are struggling to find the school behaviour policy; scribble up some smiley face symbols onto a whiteboard and you are good to go!

I developed this idea after working in three schools in three years and in no less than 14 classrooms! It was hard to establish myself in one place, I was carrying my whole life around with me. Each of the schools used their own behaviour systems and policies that were so complicated to follow that by the time I started to get my head around them, I had been teaching a full term.

I survived by creating my own system. It's so simple that it works regardless of any behaviour policy in any school.

☺ Praise

☺ Warning

☹ Concern

How it works:

- It really is as easy as it looks. The visual temperament of the faces and their associated emotion represents how you view students' behaviour.
- Either make your own set of smiley faces and stick them up on your wall, or using ICT, invent your own system for tracking behavioural events in your classroom.

Here are a few student scenarios:

- Sian Always-In-The-Library displays some excellent subject understanding and her name is added below the 'praise' smiley face. She is rewarded during or after the lesson if her name remains on display.
- Kyle Cheeky-So-and-So pulls out a pack of playing cards during the lesson and receives a warning. His name is added to the 'warning' smiley face symbol.
- Mohammed Could-Do-Better provided some outstanding homework, but has since been off-task despite your reminders. His name is scrubbed off the 'praise' smiley face section of the display.
- Derrick Has-Problems-At-Home arrives four minutes late, without an excuse and his name goes quietly up alongside the 'concern' smiley face. This is followed up during or immediately after the lesson.

Taking it further

Create a set of A6 laminated flashcards with the symbols colour coded, red, amber and green. Attach them to your whiteboard or carry them in your teacher planner.

Bonus idea

Take 3 photographs of yourself that represent the following emotions: happy, disgruntled and sad. Print out the photos (human-face size) and glue or laminate the images onto cardboard. Now place the three images onto your classroom wall. You now have your own visual representation of 'Smiley Faces'!

Padlocked

"It's a battle just getting through one activity with my bottom set Year 9s – they're always interrupting me!"

Padlock your lessons tight against classroom interruptions. The padlocked idea signifies a clenched fist on learning and the learner, tolerating zero intrusion.

Outstanding teaching and learning should proceed without any interruption. This is not an easy feat for challenging classroom environments. If only you could 'actually' padlock students, then this would be a practical idea we could seriously take further! Instead, I suggest you place a Behaviour Event Box in a corner of your classroom. Padlock it, and inform students that you will post something into it every time you are disappointed with their behaviour. Open it up at the end of each term to reveal how their behaviour has collectively improved (or not!) during the term. This will also be a great memento to you, during those frustrating moments.

How do you know you are padlocked?

1 Students' attitudes to learning must be exemplary and they make every effort to ensure that others learn and thrive in an atmosphere of respect and dignity.
2 There is a very high level of engagement, courtesy, collaboration and cooperation.
3 There is a systematic, consistently applied approach to behaviour management, which makes a strong contribution to an exceptionally positive climate for learning.

#Padlocked

But that's another story!

"Telling stories improves behaviour. Fact."

Grab your students' attention with a story. They'll be putty in your hands as you drip feed more of the tale as the lesson progresses.

Lessons that are well pitched use imaginative teaching strategies. A colleague once told me to 'tell the students a story'. I knew this subconsciously; but until I heard it out loud, I'd never really tried to make it part of my lesson planning. Outstanding lessons are well judged by a great teacher, often using different methodologies to engage and enthuse. These can be deployed with more and more confidence as your experience develops. I have discovered the secret lies in supplying the intrigue at the start of the lesson and delivering the remaining parts throughout the rest of the lesson.

Capture students' imagination by:

- Dressing up in character.
- Presenting a bogus email/letter to the class outlining government changes ahead
- Using puppets!
- Introducing news alerts at the end of each lesson, thus engaging students and ensuring they cannot wait for the next installment.
- Pairing up with a colleague and asking them to burst into your classroom to re-enact an objective.

Teaching tip

Why not introduce a Mr Benn style portal for a character change or a Jackanory approach to a sequence of lessons.

I have *my* GCSEs...

"...so I don't care whether you do your homework or not."

Expose your own examination results to the class. Share what successes and failures you encountered as a 16 year old. Make it real!

Teaching tip

Imparting advice about subjects you were not good at and how you overcame those barriers can offer credibility when discussing issues with students who don't grasp the importance of gaining qualifications.

'I have *my* GCSEs' is often heard in classrooms, corridors and playgrounds throughout the country when dealing with poor behaviour. Never spoken with any positive connotation, I often question the need for using such a statement in discussions with students. Allow me to suggest how this could be done in a positive context. Okay, some practical work for you here:

1 Dig out your own school qualifications. No, seriously, put this book down and do it.
2 I mean it. Put this book down now and go digging through your chest of drawers. I'm not going to continue until you get up off your backside and search around for that elusive set of qualifications!
3 You should now be holding your results in one hand and this book in the other.
4 Right, look through all your qualifications. Reflect on what was; what could have been.
5 How did you fare in your teaching subject? Your second subject? Is there any match between your first qualifications and your post-16 qualifications? Your degree?
6 Was it an easy journey? Where did you fail? What happened? Why? What inspired you to carry on?
7 Aha! It's the answer to the last question that you need to share with your students.
8 Take a photocopy of your qualifications into the classroom. Be ready to share your success and failure stories.

Bonus idea ★

Present your results as an assembly. Use the information to highlight personal triumphs and failures. Here is my version for the world to see online at: www.bloomsbury.com/TeacherToolkit

Teaching behaviour: the 'what'

"One size does not fit all."

When teaching behaviour, remember that every student has a wealth of prior experiences that affect their behaviour, and no two students' experiences will be the same.

We all know that children learn behaviour from an extremely early age and form their own opinions about good and bad, acceptable and unacceptable behaviour. In a world full of rules, children can adapt to conform to or rebel against the scenarios they meet.

Imagine a very young child and fast-forward their life ten years. Place them in your classroom. Consider that this young student (let's call him Johnny Bookless) has accumulated a range of life experiences full of bumps and bruises, and has not learnt societal conformity at home. He typically pushed the boundaries in his former classrooms. So, how do you go about teaching him and the class your behavioural expectations?

1 Having established your routines for the group, share the classroom boundaries.
2 Explain how you would like Johnny Bookless to behave. (This is the 'what'.)
3 Insist that there will be no exceptions.
4 Repeat numbers 1-3.
5 Repeat numbers 1-3 again and then move on.
6 Share the consequences with Johnny Bookless. (This is the learning.)
7 Action the consequences where applicable.
8 Repeat numbers 6-7 above.
9 Look for every possibility to praise and reward. (This completes how it is taught.)
10 Repeat number 9.

Taking it further

You will modify your practice over the years and from school to school. Share your behaviour strategies with colleagues; observe what other teachers do. Perhaps observe Johnny Bookless in another subject area.

#Behave

Managing behaviour: the 'why'

"Effective teachers will plan thoughtfully and perceptively for discipline issues." Bill Rogers.

When managing behaviour always clearly explain your expectations. Implementing a behaviour system and managing it consistently can reduce low-level disruption.

Teaching tip

Behaviour management strategies must be clear so that all students can understand them easily and they must be applied consistently. People make mistakes though. If you get something wrong when implementing your behaviour management strategy, remember to apologise.

Your behaviour management strategy is the system that you have in place to reward or punish any behaviour (good or bad). When students are taught how to behave visibly and systematically, they respond very well and can work cooperatively with each other. Coaching student conduct will contribute to a positive climate for learning, allowing rapid progress to take place. Use your body and non-verbal cues to signal intent. For example, if a student interrupts you, this can be swiftly rebuffed with a hand lifted up, a raised eyebrow, a tilt of the head and a brief pause.

1 Keep your language clear, firm and straightforward. Verbal sanctions can be delivered one-to-one with students in a quiet corner of the classroom.
2 Self-regulate your choice of vocabulary. Instead of 'I need you to' say 'you need to'.
3 Ensure that you follow the behaviour code of conduct for the school and your own classroom, unfailingly.
4 Share your systems and procedures.
5 Always follow up classroom occurrences with the appropriate praise or sanctions.
6 Convey respect at all times.
7 If necessary, provide classroom notices or provide quiet, isolated and calm reminders when necessary.

#Behave

Modelling behaviour: the 'how'

"One of my Year 9s asked me quite bluntly, 'how come teachers are allowed to shout at us when we're not allowed to shout at them?' I had to admit, it was obviously double standards."

The first rule of modelling behaviour is to abide by your own rules and practise what you preach!

So far, we have discussed what to teach, and why to manage behaviour, but we must also consider how a teacher must model their own behaviour: the 'how'.

Unassuming strategies for modelling behaviour:

1 Share your expectations with students by engaging them and agreeing a protocol.
2 Whatever you put in place, you will need to be able to manage and model these strategies.
3 If students are expected to adhere to your behavioural expectations, then so should you as the teacher by modelling them all.
4 Know how often you will share your behaviour expectations.
5 Always focus on the primary reason. Don't go off on a tangent, or allow a secondary behaviour event to become the motivation for a sanction.
6 Keep yourself in check by ensuring that students understand the reasoning behind initial consequences.
7 And finally, be prepared to adapt your strategy to suit a different context. After all, you wouldn't tell Johnny Bookless off in the main school reception in view of visitors. If you had to, how would you do it?

Teaching tip

When in difficulty, it is a useful approach to question the student about how they would like to be treated. In doing so, you can then apply their own expectations to the situation.

(#Behave)

Supporting behaviour: 'what if'

"No man is an island. You cannot do it alone."

It's vital to support behaviour. Don't be afraid to share behavioural concerns with a critical friend. Don't always go straight up the ladder of authority for a resolution.

Supporting behaviour pulls the last three ideas together, to allow you to teach successfully and enable students to learn. By understanding how students pick up behavioural traits, we will be more aware of why they behave the way they do in certain situations. By managing behaviour strategies we ensure students are aware of what is expected of them and are aware of the consequences that will befall them if they do not meet our expectations. By modelling the behaviour we describe, we show students exactly how we want them to behave, practising what we preach. So, how do we make it all work?

The backbone for supporting behaviour:

1 Plan for praise: have a display of some kind to showcase progress, hard work, collaboration and commitment to learning.
2 Plan for sanctions: what systems do you need to use? What resources will you require? Do the systems need to be adapted to suit the lesson, or the students' age group? Will you shift the punishment thresholds? Why? How? For example, the third time a student arrives late to class having ignored all your warnings; what should you do next? Why? How will you do it? What if they still do not respond?

3 What are the alternatives? Create a one off lesson plan for praise and sanctions that inform students of how your systems will work. The time spent on this could save all sorts of headaches later.

4 Delivery: keep in mind all the rewards and sanctions your toolkit can deliver. Do the students need a reminder? If so, how often? Is your behaviour strategy on display? If you offer rewards, do you have the tools to allocate them in the lesson?

5 Streamline how you offer rewards and sanctions. Both can be delivered with genuine meaning through language. Try it. The next time a student works really hard, instead of following the school policy of offering a sticker or a credit, try going out of your way to deliver the good news in a different context. Contemplate announcing praise during an assembly or at lunch in the playground. Consider making a Friday night phone call to the student's home.

Taking it further

Ask for help. Even after 20 years, my strategies have been reinvigorated time and time again, to meet the needs of an evolving cohort. Behaviour strategies cannot sit still!

#Behave

Bonus idea

Download the five minute behaviour plan now! It has been developed to help address the frustrations that many teachers and staff have who work in schools with low-level disruption. The plan focuses on rules, routines, relationships and disciplinary interventions (rewards, sanctions and behaviour management strategies). The resource can be downloaded online at: www.bloomsbury.com/TeacherToolkit

Fix that tie!

"You've got to accentuate the positive; eliminate the negative and latch on to the affirmative; don't mess with Mr. Inbetween."

School uniform can be a major area of disagreement between students and teachers but a bit of reverse psychology and bargaining can go a long way to promoting school policy and self respect.

Uniform is an essential part of the school establishment that we have all grown to accept. Whether we believe in it or not, the uniform can be a positive foundation in terms of anti-bullying, safety and pride. However, ties (and many other factors) can be a particularly troublesome part of school uniform and they can be a source of behaviour problems and argumentative discourse for any classroom teacher. If your school does not have a uniform, then you can apply the same principle to pencil cases, calling out in class, homework submission and so on.

Allow me to share the positive techniques I've used to address uniform woes.

- Stand at your classroom door and provide each student with a score out of ten for the quality of their tie or uniform attire. They do not need to know why this level is provided, perhaps keep it a secret, and allow students to start deciphering the code.
- Or, when students need a pencil, I ask in return, usually in a loud and obvious whisper, for a tie adjustment in order to meet their request. If they do not oblige, a pencil can be given in exchange for a sanction. In my experience nine times out of ten, the student will opt for the tie adjustment!

#TieFix

Homework

Part 6

Every lesson, every day

"Off-the-wall, yet planned, homework activities."

Consider including some activities that do not need to be assessed when you set homework. Yes, homework without marking!

Teachers dread setting homework for many reasons. The main ones are fear of collecting huge piles of marking, chasing up incomplete work and setting sanctions for students that submit anything! I don't condone the avoidance of setting homework. In fact, I advocate setting frequent and inspiring homework. But it must be a prerequisite that homework does not burden teachers with excessive marking. The aim is that when mentioned, the word inspires students to take part and want to return to class with responses to demonstrate learning.

Homework ideas that can be set every lesson, every day, with no need for marking:

- Watch the six o'clock news and report back, verbally, one of the headline stories.
- If you were headteacher, what would you want to see improved in this school.
- Take a photo of a shop sign and suggest how you could improve it.
- Interview a local shopkeeper about what history they know of the local area.
- Calculate the time taken to travel from your home to school, using a bicycle, car or bus.
- Write a mandate to become Prime Minister.
- Describe how you would live off ten pounds for a week. Explain your decisions.
- Open the dictionary at random and learn how to spell and define one new word.

#OOHs

My greatest mistake

"Mistakes are welcome in an outstanding classroom."

Emphasise to your students that mistakes are useful and in your classroom, they are welcome.

To encourage risk taking in your own practice, I would advocate a slip-up classroom culture. What I mean by this is: gaffs, duds and draft copies of work. If students accept that their first attempt at their homework will always be given the status of 'first draft', then once feedback is provided, students can respond to their draft and act upon their mistakes.

Why mistakes are welcome in an outstanding classroom?

1 It teaches us to accept that work is never perfect.
2 We develop and evolve to be less fearful.
3 We learn problem solving strategies in order to cope with feedback.
4 Recognising mistakes means we are progressing.
5 Having a positive mindset will disseminate and embed itself into our everyday practice.

My greatest homework-related mistakes:

1 Setting homework for the sheer hell of it!
2 Forgetting that not all homework tasks need to be marked.
3 Failing to provide students with differentiated homework tasks.
4 Spending significant chunks of my lessons chasing up homework.
5 Not spending enough time or thought creating exciting and enriching homework.

Teaching tip

Create a huge A3 colourful sign for your classroom wall. Add the following text 'Mistakes are welcome!'

Taking it further

What homework could you provide as a longer term assignment that involves cross-curricular references that students are working on, developing and redrafting over a half term or longer? Look at forthcoming events on the school calendar and think carefully how you could tie them into your own homework-setting.

#Mistakes

It's different this time

"Miss, can I hand my homework in early?"

Consider setting at least two different types of homework to pose the concept of free choice but discreetly offering differentiated and targeted activities for individual students.

Get into the habit of always giving students a choice between at least two homework tasks. I've found that this gives a much higher chance of students attempting something and returning completed work to me. So, how do you attempt setting more than one homework task? One of the strategies that I have used for over 15 years is to provide students with a piece of paper to glue into their student planners. That includes a list of your homework options. Number each of them and increase the level of difficulty.

The complexity of language can be increased to match the different grade descriptors; key knowledge, skills and understanding. You can praise students accordingly to the level of challenge they set themselves and monitor student choices in your classroom and gauge popular choices and adapt future tasks accordingly. The occasional hint to individual students to choose the appropriate level can also be made with a wink and a smile.

Choice One: Complete a range of initial design ideas for a healthy snack to be sold in the school canteen. Ensure your ideas are coloured and labelled.

Choice Two: Complete a range of initial design ideas for a healthy snack that could be sold in the school canteen but also in a packed-lunch box set. Ensure your ideas are annotated and that you complete market research with your selected target market.

Taking it further

Consider students selecting their own tasks. Download my homework sheet template online at: www.bloomsbury.com/ TeacherToolkit

Bonus idea ★

For fun, create two or three homework tasks that can be set for the end of term or for busy periods of the year when there are distractions going on that can sometimes affect the routine of timetabled homework. Come up with a bizarre ritual or game for choosing this week's homework task.

A deadline is a deadline

"STOP PRESS!"

Create an authentic newsroom context for student work and introduce true external accountability.

One area of the world, outside the classroom, where the word deadline has real meaning, is the newsroom. In news publishing and broadcasting, the thrill of the deadline is real, and the excitement that comes from achieving high standards of accuracy at the same time as having to meet fixed, non-negotiable deadlines can be addictive.

For a term, transform the classroom into a newsroom. Divide students into two competitive media companies, each of which have to develop a print, radio and television arm. In the weeks leading up to their live broadcast and publication date, give them a series of assignments, each with their own deadline. Tell them a missed deadline means it will not be published and counts against their company.

The main task of the companies is to build an audience for their live broadcast. Promise them that audience figures will be counted in the final outcome, so encourage them to get their parents and friends to watch! Assessment of the students' work should focus on the key learning outcomes: writing, speaking and presenting for audience and purpose; high accuracy in spelling, diction, punctuation and grammar; sophisticated appreciation of content matters such as bias, objectivity, evidence and veracity of sources.

On broadcast date, publish the newspaper articles, radio broadcasts and television newscast on the internet.

by @Edutronic_Net

Teaching tip

Samples of work from a Year 8 class can be found online at www.bit.ly/ChristopherWaugh, including a live video stream, two radio streams and a range of newspaper articles.

Spit it out! (What? Why? How?)

"What? Why? How?"

I use this in everything I do, from communications with staff, to lesson planning and student feedback; I can't live without this theory and I suggest it's probably the one idea I'd like you to take away with you!

Teaching tip

Place 'What? Why? How?' signs all around your classroom and on all student worksheets.

We have a tendency to fixate on the 'what' element of learning, forgetting about the 'why' and 'how'. If we keep reminding ourselves by using the What? Why? How? formula we will begin to engage students in the more sophisticated processes of analysis and reasoning, therefore enabling students to 'spit it out' and attain to a deeper level of education. For each question, students write a short sentence alongside their work answering the What? Why? and How? questions. Alternatively, they can use the questions to form verbal feedback responses. The formula can be used at any part of the lesson, not just for homework activities (see Idea 10 for how it can improve your marking).

Answers like 'because my teacher told me to do it' or 'because this will help me achieve a higher grade' are banned. Students must really analyse why each activity helps their learning and understanding, as well as how they tackled it.

Bonus idea   ★

Consider making 'What? Why? How?' your teaching mantra in all lessons. Insist students ask their peers these questions. Don't accept any work without it completed!

- **What?** What are you doing? What work is on this page? What have you learnt today?
- **Why?** Why have you done this work? Why are you doing it this way?
- **How?** How did you complete the task? How will this help you?

#WWH

Takeaway homework

"Sir, I'd like a takeaway homework please."

How can you provide on-the-spot homework for all your students? Consider a takeaway menu or lottery box with pre-planned tasks for students to select on a lucky-dip basis.

Imagine a takeaway menu. The dishes on offer are divided into sections and are numbered with a short description. There are also special offers and seasonal information. Translate this idea to takeaway homework:

1 Write a list of 50 homework ideas for a key stage, project or year group.
2 Divide them into sections. For example, research, development, evalution.
3 Add in a few seasonal homeworks to complete, for example at Easter and Christmas.
4 Decide if you want to place the homeworks in a sequential order using a subject specific, assessment criteria or just number them at random.
5 Add one statement describing each homework and what is needed.
6 Make sure each homework task can literally be read there and then and is a takeaway; it should require no further guidance.
7 Decide on what method you will use to display this resource. A huge banner? A tombola? Using the interactive whiteboard and a lottery number selector? Simply laminated and stuck to the wall?
8 Consider setting one random takeaway homework task once a half term.

Teaching tip

There will always be a time when you either need to pull a last minute homework idea out of nowhere, or those delightful moments when students ask you for more work to complete at home. Make sure you have your takeaway list accessible at all times.

Taking it further

Consider adding all your takeaway homework tasks to this online random selector: www.bit.ly/ TakeawayHomework.

#TakeawayHmk

Get online!

"A different way of setting homework."

Using an online platform for setting and collecting homework is a great alternative to carting around mountains of exercise books!

I've recently started using an online platform for setting student homework. It's a fantastic tool for monitoring and tracking homework but it's also invaluable because it allows the entire teaching staff, as well as parents, to access homework set across the school. It's ideal for cross-curricular enrichment opportunities too. Digital platforms are in plentiful supply. There's ShowMyHomework, Fronter, Frog, and lots more. However, these are all subscription-based platforms that schools need to pay for. Below is a free alternative.

1 Create your own Google account.
2 Access the Google 'Drive', which is the name for the area where you can store all your online documents.
3 Either 'create' or 'upload' a document containing all the homework tasks.
4 Visit www.bitly.com and create your own account.
5 Copy the Google document hyperlink and paste it into the bitly.com website.
7 Edit the weblink address name to make it easier to find. For example, www.bit.ly/Year7Food. The link can be emailed to parents and tutors, and students can record the website address in the planners.

Student-led homework

"My students always groan when I mention the H word, but since I started giving them a choice in the matter they've become much more enthusiastic!"

Keep your students on their toes every lesson by getting them to decide their own homework tasks.

Students will always surprise you. No matter how long you've been teaching, you'll definitely come across a few things that you didn't expect. Getting my students to choose their own homework was certainly one of those moments for me. Initially I was sceptical, I scoffed and I thought they'll just decide that the homework is to watch television or to have a kickabout with a football on the way home; but then came the surprise. The class and I put 'homework' on trial.

I asked the class to organise themselves into a classroom courtroom; they split themselves into the prosecution versus defence teams, there was a judge and members of the jury. Then I asked them to discuss and argue the pros and cons of setting homework, in general and specifically about the tasks that were on offer that week. The judge mediates the opening statements, conducts cross-examinations and interrogates any witnesses. At the end, the jury is asked to come to a verdict.

Not only did the class find in favour of homework, they also discussed and amended the homework tasks I'd chosen in ways I hadn't expected.

This idea will hopefully inspire you to let your students take the reins on homework too!

Teaching tip

Why not use this idea as a selection process for students choosing their next scheme of work?

Taking it further

Other ideas of student-led homework: give students a camera and let them take it home or use it at lunchtime to answer the questions you set as homework. Then get them to explain their decisions and photos in the next lesson. Set an open ended question and get students to assign each other different ways of answering it. Tell them to be as creative as they can: create a poster, a PowerPoint presentation, via Pictionary style drawing, even through song, dance or even mime!

The jury is out

"Guilty as charged!"

Make sure you mark every single piece of work and offer feedback.

We probably manage 100% homework collections once or twice in our careers; typically the collection and completion of homework depends on what was on the television the night before, what homework has been set in other subjects and how bothered you can be to collect it in!

Typical excuses include:

1 'I've lost it!'
2 'We moved house at the weekend and I've left it at my Gran's house.'
3 'My printer isn't working!'

How to deal with the excuse:

1 'No problem; (smile) we can do it together after the lesson.'
2 'That's fine, (mimic a phone to your ear) let's call Gran after the lesson to confirm it's safe.'
3 'My printer is working, let's print it off now.'

Avoid high levels of confrontation that lead to the issue taking over the learning.

1 Embed routines for setting and collecting homework. Be transparent and consistent with rewards and sanctions. Even if you have to set over 50% detentions or rewards, make sure you do it.
2 Keep calm when students let you down. Don't allow it to affect your emotions and turn what potentially could be a great lesson into a dour and sombre affair.
3 Collect homework discreetly during the lesson rather than during the register. Any homework excuses will only delay a dynamic start to any lesson!

#Order

Questioning

Part 7

Target practice

"Practice makes perfect!"

Plan what you'll be asking your students in the lesson and choose different questions to suit each student's ability.

Target practice is one of my favourite questioning strategies and one of the most popular resources I've shared online. This idea is all about targeting your questions appropriately and exactly for each student. It is perfect for planning questions for schemes of work, lesson planning and homework setting.

Differentiated questioning uses the Bloom's Taxonomy structure of higher order thinking to formulate a template for planned questioning. It can be used to plan a series of questions over time, or to build up a bank of questions to use within a long-term project. Understanding can also be checked systematically through effective questioning. A short example is shown below for a Year 7 Resistant Materials Technology project:

Knowledge – Level three, grade F
- What is a structure?
- What is the purpose of a bridge?
- Who designed the Empire State Building?

Comprehension – Level four, grade E
- Explain the term Triangulation.
- Describe two ways to strengthen a frame structure.
- Identify the two forces that act on a shelf when it bends.

Application – Level four +, grade E/D
- Can you combine two different materials to construct a tower?
- How have you made this?

Analysis – Level five, grade C

- Why do you think most buildings combine different materials?
- What evidence is there to suggest that a pyramid is a stable shape?
- Why do you think it is important for structures to be able to withstand geological movements?

Synthesis – Level five/six, grade B+

- How would you change a basic beam bridge design to make it more aesthetically pleasing?
- How would you improve your bridge design to make it stronger?
- How would you change the structure of the Empire State Building based on what you know now?

Evaluation – Level six/seven, grade B/A

- What is your opinion of the structures designed in the 1920s in New York City?
- How effective was your design when testing weight distribution?
- How accurate were your measurements?

Consider 'all, most and some'. If all students had to answer a question above, what question would it be for your class? What type of question would you expect most to answer? And finally, what question would you expect some to answer as a challenge?

Can you translate the above to suit a project you teach in your own subject area?

Taking it further

This idea can be made even easier to implement by colour-coding the questions written up on your whiteboard or classroom wall. Over time, students can colour-code themselves by attempting the questions based on the coding/assessment.

Show off

"If you break him in half, you'll see 'Outstanding' written all the way through, like a stick of rock."

When did you last read the guidance for what makes an Outstanding lesson?

'Show off' refers to lessons that you teach that are not observed by your line manager, nor the senior leadership team, or even Ofsted; those lessons that you teach day-in-day-out on a Friday afternoon, or towards the end of term when you and the kids are exhausted, that are darn good, but nobody sees!

Not sure which part of your teaching to develop in order to be Outstanding? Use the following Outstanding criteria, any section, as a questioning checklist to ask yourself for everyday outstanding teaching.

Subject knowledge and use of assessment:

- Is your subject knowledge up to date? Really? Even with cross-curricular references?
- How do you assess prior learning systematically and accurately?
- Understanding is checked systematically through effective questioning?
- Do you anticipate interventions?
- Are systems in place to involve all students in reading and responding to feedback, as well as acting on feedback?
- Are your learners confident and critical in assessing their own and others' work?
- Do your students regularly set themselves meaningful targets for improvement?

Teaching:

- Are the tasks you set challenging? Do they match students' needs accurately?

- Do you pitch your lessons well and use imaginative teaching strategies that leave colleagues in awe?
- Are your expectations consistently high?
- Is the support you offer appropriate and does it have a notable impact on progress?
- Do you probe and tease out misconceptions? Are all learners enthusiastic and keen to move on?
- Is your teaching of literacy, numeracy and other skills exceptional?
- Do you involve your teaching assistants in planning and is there good communication between you?

Learning and progress:
- Do students show high levels of enthusiasm, interest, resilience, confidence and engagement?
- Are students learning exceptionally well?
- Do all students make rapid and sustained progress? How do you know? Evidence please?

Homework:
- Do you set appropriate and regular homework that contributes very well to students' learning?
- Does the homework you set have a choice of activities?

Attitudes to learning and behaviour:
- Are students' attitudes to learning exemplary?
- Do students make every effort to ensure that others learn and thrive in an atmosphere of respect?
- Is there a very high level of engagement, courtesy, collaboration and cooperation in your classroom?
- Do your lessons proceed without interruption (throughout)?
- Is there a systematic, consistently applied approach to behaviour management?

Taking it further

Treat all the lessons you teach as if you were being observed. Do you think you could make at least one or two of the questions listed in this idea your own target for this term?

#ShowOff

So, what did I say you had to do?

"What's the point?"

Consider the possible outcomes for asking this question after you've delivered your instructions. Can you think of a positive one? No. I thought so!

I think there are two possible outcomes when you ask, 'So, what did I say you had to do?' The first is that the students repeat back to you to confirm what they have to do. Rather than being worthwhile, all this achieves is reducing valuable learning time! The second outcome is silence or mumbling, confirming that only one or two students know what to do and suggesting that an inadequate set of instructions have just been given.

Therefore, this question is best avoided at all costs as it is a waste of time. So, how can we steer clear of using this question in our teaching and avoid such a weak questioning technique for students regurgitating knowledge?

The answer is to make your students engage in your objectives for each lesson.

- Cut up your lesson objectives into various sizes asking the students to unscramble the words and put them in order. This will get your students decoding the objectives physically, mentally and visually, thus increasing opportunities for information to stick.
- Ensuring your instructions are delivered using the MINT strategy (Idea 90).
- Make sure your information is not overcomplicated. Use the KISS approach (Idea 91).

Pose, pause, pounce, bounce

"Teasing out students' thinking is far more important than moving onto the next stage of any lesson."

Probe, probe, probe. Do not be afraid to allow students to be comfortable with being stuck.

This simple Assessment for Learning questioning technique could revolutionise your teaching! Use this technique to get students analysing, evaluating and critiquing each other's answers, as well as learning how to become unstuck by themselves.

1 **Pose** – Provide a question, ensure that you ask the students to remain reflective.
2 **Pause** – Ask the class to contemplate the question, consider their answer, think about it and then think some more.
3 **Pounce** – Ask a student for his or her answer. Insist that the answer comes from the student you chose, directly and fast!
4 **Bounce** – Ask another student immediately after the pounce response about their opinion of the first student's answer.

The technique gets students thinking about their thinking. They are encouraged to engage with their peers' thought processes too in order to tease out why they think the way they do. It doesn't matter if the answer is correct or not, the aim is to evaluate thinking processes and develop responses. It's a great way to get teachers to take risks in the classroom too.

Teaching tip

Download my detailed and very popular PowerPoint resource online at: www.bloomsbury.com/TeacherToolkit that links this questioning technique to the characters of Winnie The Pooh! Are you a Tigger in the classroom?

#PPPB

To question or not to question

"If you want to change the dynamic of knowledge and power in your classroom, ban questions!"

What would happen in your classroom if you banned all questions? How would you cope? How much do you rely on the traditional question and response strategy?

Teaching tip

Look at your lesson objective, and write down the five questions you might ask to effectively assess if your students have learned from the lesson. See if you can change any of these questions into something else, such as a tiny game, task or response from students. By removing the question and response strategy, how can you deepen learning and understanding?

In my experience, the majority of questions from students are either to find out more information or to clarify instructions. Questions posed by teachers are either asking students to identify an answer in the teacher's head, or to assess if students know what they need to do. What would happen if we banned questions from both teachers and students? Read on to discover how to answer these questions without asking them!

What strategies could you put in place to find out what the students want to know?

- Install a voting box.
- Stick Post-its on a wall.
- Turn students' desks into whiteboards.

How could you ensure students had enough instructions to carry out work?

- Use traffic lights to self-assess students' understanding.
- Create a system of communicating with silent signals.
- Get students to pair up for support.

Why do you want the students to play 'guess what's in my head'? How else could they answer?

- Use the Roman voting system of thumbs up or thumbs down.
- Use a method of list ticking.
- Get students to hold up their fingers with their responses.

One of the most effective questioning strategies I have ever used is to put the student's name first, rather than last. 'Ross, why might we use a cog in this model?' allows Ross to know that this question is just for him and tunes the other students into his answer.

Assessment of a group's understanding can often be used as an effective plenary strategy by asking five relevant questions, consisting of one for the lower ability, three generalist questions and one for the higher ability. These questions need to be targeted and specific, and with enough planning, can be carried out in very little time and be incredibly useful for diagnostic purposes.

by @MrLockyer

Taking it further

There is a fabulous questioning grid I'd recommend you look up by geography teacher @JohnSayers, which helps you to formulate deeper questioning. I use it all the time! www.bit.ly/ JohnSayers

Bonus idea

Probe deeper with your questioning. As John says (see taking it futher), ask students "why did you give that answer?" Try using the Socratic circle questioning 6-step process: clarify; challenge assumption; evidence for argument; viewpoints and perspectives; implications and consequences and finally, question the question.

Robotic talk

"Embrace your inner robot!"

Do you ever feel like a broken record-player, a parrot or a robot repeating instructions over and over again?

I'm sure, like me, you've been a little frustrated at times with individual students and certain classes that know how to push your buttons. It can feel like you've tried everything and you're at the end of your tether. For me, this usually stems from repeating instructions time and time again like a parrot or a robot.

On one of these days the idea struck me to show the class my frustrations. I altered my voice and droned on in my best robot impersonation, complaining about having to repeat myself. The funny thing was that the tactic really worked to engage the class! They all quietened down and listened. So shake up how you speak and how you say things. There are a plethora of possibilities here; but here are my top suggestions:

1 Try talking like Yoda from Star Wars. 'Try it, you must!'
2 Put on a different accent, perhaps Cockney or Geordie.
3 Try singing your instructions to the class.
4 Use your inner robot; combine it with your best robotic dance moves too!
5 Perhaps for fun, consider passing on the instructions as 'Chinese whispers'.
6 Ask your students to respond in their own impressions, the robot, different accents, or even their best impression of you!

#RoboQs

Observations

Part 8

Reducing teacher talk

"You talk less; the students talk more!"

A lengthy lecture from a teacher isn't the best use of your time. Read on for ways to drown out the sound of your own voice.

Picture the scene; your line manger has agreed to visit your classroom and observe the teaching and learning taking place and as if on cue, they arrive and voila! You burst into a song of dialogue and soliloquy. Does this sound familiar? This is not what teaching is about and certainly a flaw in the observation and appraisal process (inadvertently dictated by Ofsted). Even saying all the right things during an observation reduces the opportunities for students to share and in turn it can hinder their learning. Try using the following strategies to keep your own mouth shut during lessons and let your students take the lead.

- Start the lesson with a video clip and a question to spark an initial debate.
- Provide students with an answer and ask them to come up with the appropriate questions.
- Break up a particular piece of text onto separate sheets. Students then have to then work together to put the information back into its original order.
- Get your students to lead part of the lesson. This could involve getting one of them to explain concepts to the rest of the class or leading a group discussion in a starter activity.
- Use short bursts of discussion in student pairs, rather than teacher leading.
- Imagine you cannot talk! Think of different ways you could communicate. Perhaps employ a student translator to decipher your actions.

Teaching tip

Be part of the debate here: www.bit.ly/TeacherTalk

Taking it further

Give students a stopwatch and ask them to time your talking. Set yourself a challenge of only talking for ten minutes per lesson. Make it even harder by reducing the time you're allowed!

#TeacherTalk

Student teachers

"WARNING: This idea should not only be delivered in lesson observations."

Encourage your students to take more responsibility for their own learning.

Chris Watkins from the Institute of Education asked 'what do you think happens most often?'

1 Learning without teaching?
2 Teaching without learning?

It's a good question. I would put my money on option one being more akin to an Outstanding classroom. Would you? How could you encourage learning without teaching? In essence, students leading their own learning and becoming more of a teacher type learner in the classroom.

Display some large question marks around your classroom with questions hidden behind them. Inform the students that these are questions that you do not know the answers to and that you would like them to provide you with the answer during this lesson.

More ideas for creating student teachers:

1 Embed a 'learning process' as the fundamental skill within your classroom.
2 Encourage risk taking at all costs.
3 Encourage students to tackle problems and accept that getting stuck will be normal.
4 Create opportunities for students to lead their own learning.
5 Focus on learning, not the activity.

Teaching tip

Encourage students to take risks and see problems through. Do all that you can to refrain from providing the answer. Focus tightly on the learning, the problem and the journey of becoming unstuck.

Taking it further

Encourage students to create learning journals to describe what they have learnt and the permutations this could lead to. You could provide some further higher order questions for students to consider, based on the difficulties they have overcome.

Impact!

"Being outstanding is not simply doing more good things, it's doing different things. It involves a mindset shift."

By shifting the focus from the lesson plan towards the learner you can be consistently outstanding.

Are you fed up with being told that your lesson was a good lesson, given a grade two and then in an attempt to pacify you the observer adds, 'but there were some outstanding elements'? The CPD Programme, #OutstandingIn10Plus10 was developed for all those good teachers out there who want to be outstanding. Having watched hundreds of lessons here is a quick summary of my thoughts.

Good lessons

- Learning gains = Tight
- Lesson structure = Tight
- Focuses on = The lesson plan

Lessons that require improvement

- Learning gains = Loose
- Lesson structure = Tight
- Focuses on = The activities

In outstanding lessons:

- Teachers have absolute clarity of how the knowledge and understanding are vertically integrated in their subject and expect students to work at a conceptual level.
- Teachers keep the lesson plan loose so that they can respond to learners' needs.

by @LeadingLearner

The ripple effect

"Take into account the views of colleagues, parents and students. It's all about collaboration, good feedback and a growth mindset."

Sow the seeds early. If you happen to walk past students you will be teaching later in the day, simply tell them you can't wait to teach them later on. Tell them what a great lesson you have planned.

The ripple effect hypothesis can be applied in lesson observations and your own classroom teaching. Consider the immediate effects of your actions and your students' actions. Then consider the knock on effects of this. Remember how far the ripple travels. Everything you do has the potential to ebb outwards and the benefits, or otherwise, will be far-reaching and wide across the school community.

The ripple effect can also be associated with the interview process. In particular, from teachers attending school interviews and not getting the job. Essentially, good feedback applies in all contexts. When a candidate leaves your school, even if they are unsuccessful, they will leave equipped with constructive and detailed feedback as well as advice for their next interview. These are not only powerful strategies for the candidate; they also emit a positive impression of the school. After all, experiences and feelings about a school will be summed up in one or two sentences and this can often be enough to build up or tarnish a school's reputation through word of mouth.

The context of this article originates from conversations with my current Principal.

Taking it further

Create this philosophy in your own classroom with students. The next time you need to stop the lesson and refocus behaviour, expectations, moral code and relationships with peers and parents, consider the ripple effect. It can be applied in any framework and will certainly readjust your mindset.

#PebbleDrop

Think-pair-share

"Learning to Learn: encouraging self-sufficiency in the classroom."

Use think-pair-share to train your students in the 5Rs.

Think-pair-share (TPS) is more than sharing. The concept encourages the listener to be able to share the information they have been given and demonstrate it. It is commonly implemented for all students as a model of good practice.

Use think-pair-share to train your students to be:

Resilient
• Set achievable tasks with checkpoints.

Responsible
• Make students own your classroom philosophy. Allow them to contribute to the vision and be responsible for its upkeep. Think about refreshing the ethos each term.

Reasoning
• Encourage students to be part of the routines. Students should know what is expected of them from beginning to end.

Resourceful
• Provide students with options. Not just differentiated work, but opportunities to respond with various means. For example, perform a design idea using drama!

Reflective
• Reflective practice is fair. Admit when you are wrong and encourage all students to do the same so that the learning can move on.

Improvements only!

"You will either step forward into growth or you will step back into safety." Abraham Maslow

Focus on ways of improving learning in all types of feedback.

There are so many formulae for giving feedback to students: WWW (What Went Well), EBI (Even Better If), Two stars and a wish, A Kiss and Two Kicks, I could go on for hours! But all we really need to do it emphasise the required improvements. Forget the niceties. Let's get students down to the business end of learning from the start. 'Improvements only' should not only be evident in lesson observations, thorough book scrutiny, but systematic in your daily approach to teaching and learning. Develop your own methods for applying this way of written feedback into your own subject and ask all students to apply this technique in all that they do.

We want 'improvements only', and we want those suggestions written and recorded for developmental purposes. Contemplate this proposal: keep improvements 80% recorded and 20% of all improvements, verbal.

How about creating an 'improvements only' Post-it notes wall for your lessons? Absorb students in debate and peer and self-assessment as they adorn a wall layered in a constant flurry of comments for the greater good of the class, their project, and their own self-reflection.

Teaching tip

You can adapt and extend this approach, using Idea 55. Apply a 'What if?' following the 'What?, Why?, How?' theorem and engage students to focus on improvements in all variations of feedback. Keep the positive feedback 80% verbal and 20% recorded.

Triangulation

"Make your routines so embedded that when an observer enters the room, NOTHING needs to change!"

For all observation lessons, triangulate your sources to make an informed judgement on progress.

Since the publication of the latest Ofsted framework, we have to work harder to refine and develop a classroom ethos that best meets the criteria, whilst also supporting staff in making accurate and informed observation judgments.

What we have determined is that using the following three sources can allow observers to make appropriate judgments, taking into account 'progress over time'.

1 The lesson itself, and series of lessons over the academic year.
2 Prior and current data from students, in whichever format it is provided. For example, residuals, Key Stage Two or Three data, reading tests, teacher assessments and so on.
3 Conversations with students so that you can gather vital opinions of routines, expectations and learning. You must also evidence progress over time from exercise books. Consider a book review as an observation in itself without watching the lesson. Read through the classwork evidence; the homework; self and peer-assessment; teacher assessment; redrafts and target setting.

Item three on this list is undoubtedly the most important. I'd recommend that if a lesson observation is being conducted, that the vast majority of the lesson should be spent having conversations with students and taking time to read through books and facilitate a discussion to gather evidence.

#Triangulation

Transfixed

"Work your magic to capture students imagination!"

There's a hidden performer in every teacher; use your skills to amaze and astound.

There's a hidden performer in every teacher, somewhere inside waiting to be let loose. No matter if you are a closet magician, an amateur actor or a budding comedian, use your status and position in the classroom to capture your audience and make them transfixed! My students love it when I bring a couple of magic tricks in to the classroom. It's a great way to liven up a dull lesson or to get them to open up in class more.

Transfixed strategies:

1 Tell the class a subject secret.
2 Do not view your students as listeners, but as participants. Get them involved where possible.
3 Show first; tell later.
4 Consider a different position in the classroom.
5 Add a touch of drama. Eye contact, story-telling, adapt and emphasise your body language.

Top five tips:

1 Know your students, all of them, by name.
2 Start by asking questions.
3 Use stories.
4 Use the power of the pause.
5 Be conversational and topical.

Teaching tip

Great teaching is all about effort and planning. Take time to understand the dynamics of the group and find out what they are interested in. If necessary, research the subject and do all you can to bring the content into the learning. Students will love it if you burst into a character or use slang that they recognise.

#Transfixed

Open classroom

"Open classroom: please come in!"

Creating an open door culture in your classroom will not only benefit you as a teacher but also your colleagues, the school and your student community. That's got to be a win-win situation, right?

The open classroom model is not a new idea, but many teachers are still wary of inviting colleagues into their classroom. Email, or announce in your staff briefing, what you will be teaching your students that day and invite your colleagues to come and observe you or a student at work. There's nothing big headed about that! For example:

Period one – I will be teaching Year 8 how to bake cupcakes. Come and taste them!

Period three – Year 9 will be working in groups to decode my lesson plan. Watch me teach less!

Period five – Year 7 are presenting their Henry VIII projects using song and dance. Join us in room EG02!

- Place an 'Open Classroom' sign outside your classroom to encourage your colleagues to venture inside. Find my template online at: www.bloomsbury.com/TeacherToolkit
- Pair up with a colleague and agree to visit each other's lessons during the week. Your visits could be planned or unplanned.
- Email staff inviting them to attend a class presentation and share some photos afterwards.
- Get your students to beg their form tutors to visit your lesson.
- You could even ask the caretaker to take your classroom door off its hinges for a week!

#OpenClassroom

Progress

Part 9

Building blocks

"Build with the right bricks and fill in the cracks for real progress, Ofsted or no Ofsted."

With the right foundations and meaningful feedback, making rapid and sustained progress becomes a doddle!

For all students to make 'rapid and sustained progress' the right foundations to a lesson are essential; your lessons need to have clear and focused lesson objectives (Building blocks). Objectives that are task-based are rarely useful; to complete the task is an expectation not an objective to aid progression. It is much more useful to start from the end game, the bigger picture and work backwards. Then, if you plan activities with the focus of moving towards achieving the objectives, you're onto a winner!

Get students engaged in the objectives:
• Show them the objective.
• Get them to choose or create the objective.
• Blank out keywords to get students thinking about the objective.
• Get students connected with the learning involved to give them a vested interest in working towards achieving it.

Use on-the-spot interventions to assess where students are, so you can fill in the cracks. It is essential that you plan points in the lesson where you can check the understanding of the students, rather than power on to the end of your beautifully planned lesson. You might change the direction or give more focus to a certain idea or to a group.

#BuildingBlocks

by @MsFindlater

Rapid progress

"The goalposts have moved."

Measure rapid progress in all your lessons. Treat every lesson as if you are being observed.

How do you know if students are making rapid progress in your classroom and are learning exceptionally well? Remember that rapid progress does not always have to be measured in terms of levels. It can be as simple as amassing knowledge, validating understanding, and of course, applying skill and technique in a classroom activity. We all know that the key for observations is evidencing 'progress over time'. An observational judgment is not a one-off snapshot judgment, and evidence of progress must be verified over a series of lessons.

This small idea is a model for proving rapid progress over time in every lesson. Make it a routine and adapt the idea to suit each learning objective. Learning will gradually become embedded and the process of learning will, in turn, be visible and rapid progress will become the norm. This is particularly the case for short bursts of progress, continually.

- Set your students a task to complete in three minutes.
- Invite students to mark each others' work, providing them with the necessary success criteria.
- Ask your students to redo the task now that they are aware of the success criteria.
- Measure the progress between the two tasks.

Teaching tip

Rapid progress is not a quick fix! It certainly is not something that can be achieved in a short period of time, but this idea, embedded as a routine can certainly help students make progress.

Taking it further

Read this follow up article to put this chapter in context: www.bit.ly/ RapidProgressRead.

Improving learning, not proving progress

"Lies, damned lies and statistics."

Progress in lessons is a myth! Teachers cannot prove rapid and sustained progress in one 20 minute lesson observation!

Teaching tip

Read this fabulous blog post by @KevBartle on 'The Myths of Progress within Lessons': 'Ofsted are urging us repeatedly to focus on learning ... and the mythical creature of 'progress in lessons' has become a folk-tale boogeyman.' www.bit.ly/KevBartle.

'Progress over time', 'progress in lessons'; these statements are haunting teachers and leadership teams up and down the country. Let me clarify: there is nothing to fear! Proving progress in lessons is not a requirement that has been stipulated in the latest Ofsted framework. These statements have been misinterpreted by many leadership teams. So, feel free to rip Idea 77 out of this book, photocopy it and leave it in all your senior leadership team's pigeonholes!

Bear in mind:
- Rapid and sustained progress cannot be observed in a 20 minute lesson.
- How far would you trust the long-term impact of something mastered in 20 minutes?
- Will checking if lesson objectives can be recalled in the middle and end of a lesson measure the progress of the students? Absolutely not.
- If all my students are on task does this show rapid progress? No. This is not a measure for progress.

How do you improve learning, not prove progress?
- Strengthen your own teaching by monitoring and assessing students regularly.
- Throw out the concept of 'progress over time' in a one-off snapshot lesson.
- Build links to learning from outside the classroom which match individual needs.

#20MinsObs

Risk taking

Part 10

Student Meet

"Transfer the grassroots model of sharing best practice and implement this into your classroom."

Encourage students to share their learning amongst their peers in an organised #StudentMeet!

#StudentMeet

#TeachMeet

What is a Teach Meet? Teach Meets are informal CPD gatherings of educators who are taking training into their own hands. Some call this type of event an 'unconference'; a totally flipped model of the current type of training day you may typically attend.

So, what is a Student Meet? It's the equivalent for students. It is an opportunity for students who do amazing things in their lessons every day to share ideas and celebrate their community. The students can share their learning amongst their peers in their own classroom as well as further afield. With a bit of encouragement, students can organise Student Meets themselves; perhaps using a back-channel, which is a video or audio stream that can be immediately uploaded onto the internet or school radio.

The aim is to amaze, amuse and inspire students in the classroom and across the school, and beyond. Any student, with encouragement and great classroom management, can share interesting, useful or innovative ideas in a timed presentation. Presentations can be on any classroom topic, customarily three or six minutes long. Successes, difficulties, what you are most proud of, current affairs are all great topics that could be part of a Student Meet theme.

Pedagogically speaking

"During early education, there is an emergence in the interest of reasoning and wanting to know why things are the way they are. Logic occurs later, at around 7-11 years old."

Tolerate younger students asking 'why?' Provide older students with opportunities to make decisions.

Now, one may not associate Piaget with risk taking and you may ask why I have included this topic within this section of the book. Well, Jean Piaget was a psychologist known for his epistemological studies, primarily concerned with the nature of knowledge in children. His theory of cognitive development, or simply, the nature and development of human intelligence, indicated how humans come to gradually acquire, construct, and use knowledge.

Piaget was the great pioneer of the constructivist theory of knowledge. 'Constructivism' has associations with theories of instruction. Discovery, experiential, hands-on, project-based, collaborative and task-based learning are some of the applications that base teaching and learning on constructivism.

And there it is! A reminder to us all, that knowledge (or constructivism) is constructed in children when knowledge comes into contact with existing knowledge. This type of learner can be resourceful, self-directed and innovative. I encourage you to provide ample opportunities for your students to acquire knowledge through practical activity and experience. Throw away the textbook. Throw away the worksheet. Allow them to take a computer apart; to break open a mechanical toy to see how the mechanical cogs fit together. Whatever it is, encourage students to ask why and make their own decisions.

Teaching tip

How could you integrate acquiring knowledge without using a worksheet or a textbook? No matter how stressed and pushed for time you are, do all you can to find that 'link between knowledge and discovery' by providing ample hands-on experience.

Taking it further

A good starting point to read further information on Piaget is here: www.bit.ly/JeanPiaget.

#Piaget

Breathe

"A real education will not teach you to compete; it will teach you to cooperate. It will not teach you to fight and come first. It will teach you to be creative, to be loving, to be blissful, without any comparison with the other." Osho.

If things should start to go wrong in your lesson, don't be afraid to slow things down a little.

Often, a slowly-slowly approach can, in turn, speed up learning by helping you and your students to refocus. Basic education is a discipline. When lessons start to veer off on the wrong track, the first thing to elicit is emotional intelligence.

Consider a form of pit stop meditation, the art of looking inwards. Only from looking inwards can we deal with our own emotions and rebalance our perspective.

How it works:

- Ask all your students to place their heads on the table and close their eyes. Create a simple visual picture that transports them out of the room, far away.
- Use a very simple breathing technique. Take a deep breath through the nose; hold it for ten seconds; exhale slowly through the mouth. Repeat three times.
- Ask everyone to count slowly to 30 in their heads. You set the pace and gradually reduce your counting to a whisper and eventually a nonverbal signal such as a nod.
- Ask the class to clench their fists and hold them tightly for ten seconds. Then release. Repeat three times.
- Take a micro-break. Ask all students to talk about anything other than the lesson for one minute.

#Breathe

Hit and hope

"Fake it 'til you make it!"

Teaching someone else's subject or class can be tough, especially if you're not all that familiar with the subject, but believe in yourself and set strong foundations from the start and you'll always remain one step ahead!

Teaching relies on you always being adaptable and ready for anything. Experience helps, but there are times when you may be called upon to fill any gap and take on any guise. 'Hit and hope' takes into account all those times when you've had to think on your feet!

A good place to start is to believe in you! I'm not being sarcastic or motivationally sycophantic; I mean in the acting and performing sense. 'Fake it 'til you make it' allows the students to accept you as their teacher more quickly. Even if you are a teacher within the same school, students might still see how far they can push you as a 'cover' teacher.

So, how can you put this right?

- Set expectations very high from the outset.
- Sweat the small stuff. Do not shy away from tackling obstacles that will hinder learning.
- Discuss your own experiences and make the subject real.
- If you know you will be covering lessons prepare a catalogue of ideas that you can use in various subjects time and time again.

And to make it outstanding?

- Ask students for feedback. Implement their thoughts the very next lesson.
- Do your research! Study as much as you can about the students and subject.
- If it's not your subject area, plan, plan, plan!

Taking it further

I once observed an outstanding ICT lesson that involved not one use of a single computer. How? By, engaging students in a physically challenging and probing dialogue. Regardless of subject, expert use of questioning probes understanding and teases out misconceptions. You are experienced enough to keep asking probing questions to facilitate a healthy discussion.

#HaH

Desultory days

"Just go with the flow."

Inform the class that you will not be providing any answers for the entire lesson! Take a step back, trust your instincts and allow the natural progression of the lesson to take its course.

Sometimes we all just need to relax. We all have those desultory days in the classroom when we are feeling tired, over-observed, maybe it's near the end of term or we've had the week from hell. Desultory teaching frequently exists in my own classroom, but it is not an excuse for lack of effort. It's more a reminder to permit myself to trust the natural progression of a lesson, my own experience and my teaching style. A teaching style that spotlights the learning, not the activity.

But how do you ensure these desultory moments are outstanding?

- First, let's forget all routines that require your verbal direction. These should already be shared and rooted as typical classroom expectations. Students will naturally fall within your classroom expectations, just by you being there – don't panic!
- State categorically from the start that you will be working less than they are and that any form of praise will be provided to them on the basis that they have worked a lot harder than normal.
- Take a seat, but not at your desk. Keep moving around and sit at each student's table, working with them closely. Listen, rather than talk.
- Adopt Idea 55. Make sure all that you ask of students, is: what? why? And how?

#RandomRisks

Visualise!

"Make memories stick!"

Use a visualiser to display all kinds of weird and wonderful artefacts in your classroom.

It was sometime in 1990 that I first came across the concept of a visualiser. It's a brilliant teaching approach for providing live demonstrations without necessarily having students crowding around the teacher's desk. That was at Edge Hill University as part of an industrial experience for sixth form students, almost a quarter of a century ago!

Many years later, we've moved on from the camcorder attached to a tripod, which is linked up via various unwieldy wires to a television screen. It was awkward and cumbersome; but as a student I never forgot what I observed. It made a classroom memory stick for a lifetime.

Today, I cannot live without some form of visualisation in my own classroom. Over the years, as ICT has slowly consumed our environments, visualisers have evolved from a clunky overhead projectors, to microscopic cameras connected via USB ports and more recently, to interactive whiteboard with all the latest touchscreen technology.

How it works:
You can get your hands on pretty cheap and cheerful visualisers online, the Point-2-View camera from Ipevo, for example, (www.ipevo.com) is about £50 and is fantastic! I've just secured 100 free for all my teaching staff! Try to find yourself one that is portable, that can snap photographs and can zoom in on detail.

Taking it further

Be creative about what you display with your visualiser; examples of students' work, strange objects or whatever exciting prize you're offering for the highest mark in today's assessment! Make the visualiser a regular feature in your lesson.

Bonus idea

Have timed photographs of work captured so that students' progress can be demonstrated.

#StuckOnYou

Ends of lessons

Part 11

Time wasting

"My wall clock stopped and I lost all concept of time! I nearly sent my class home ten minutes early!"

Outstanding time filler ideas for those lessons where you finish a wee bit early!

During a lesson observation if you ever release students too early, take note of your timings and pace. Create your own list of last-minute time filler activities so you can pull ideas out of the hat to suit the context of the class.

Have you ever misread your watch or wall clock and finished your lesson off too early? I have. A slight distraction of thought and you suddenly discover that you're about to release 20-30 students out into the corridors five minutes early! Here are some five minute time filler strategies for use with any class and any subject:

- Discuss a topic from today's news.
- If you were Prime Minister, what would you do?
- If you were headteacher, what would you keep in this school? What would you get rid of?
- Mastermind. And your specialist subject is?
- Make the teacher say yes or no.

Lesson related ideas:

- The flying aeroplane technique: two groups on opposite sides of the classroom, each group writes down on the model plane what they have learnt today, then flings it to the other team. The other team catches, opens and reads the plane, then flies their own.
- Create a quick keyword spelling test or a subject quiz.
- Discuss what you will be studying next week, next term, next year.
- Ask only closed questions. They can be yes or no questions, agree or disagree or maybe some silly ones. Get students to move to areas of the classroom.

Phew!

"You're tired; the students are tired. Everyone is tired!"

Make sure you look after yourself; an exhausted teacher won't be able to get the best out of 30 exhausted students, especially come the end of the lesson.

We all know teaching can be gruelling, especially during the exam season, or when big coursework deadlines are looming, not to mention things like Ofsted. But, it's vital that we look after ourselves so that we are fully prepared to meet our least favourite challenges head on and keep momentum going right to the end of the lesson.

Here are my top staff well-being tips:

1 You cannot beat a good nights rest. Get to bed early. Yes, I mean before nine o'clock!
2 Breathe. Breathe in slowly through the nose. Hold it for ten seconds; then exhale slowly through the mouth.
3 If you move between classrooms, walk more slowly than usual. You can be forgiven for being 30 seconds later than you'd normally be. Taking it slowly will allow you to gather a bit more perspective.

Here are my top well-being tips for students:

1 Every so often ask your students to take time out. Get them to place their heads gently on the table. Ask them to close their eyes and reflect on the day's learning for 30 seconds.
2 Encourage healthy eating as part of your lesson plan. Offer segments of fruit and water to promote active thinking and learning.
3 Loosen up the rules now and then especially during long terms and dark winter days.

Taking it further

During your most stressful periods try something new: lead your class in some calming meditation. A brief escape from the worries and fears that surround us can do wonders to clear our minds and actually make our work more productive and more rewarding.

#Phew

109

The five minute lesson evaluation

"Reflect, review and consider."

Use the five minute lesson evaluation, along with the five minute lesson plan as a complimentary planning tool for lesson reflection.

Having spent many hours working with undergraduate trainee teachers, I was finding myself repeating the same advice year after year, 'create a picture in your head of what you see the students doing during the lesson'. Then I came across the five minute lesson plan. I had found the perfect model to aid planning to help achieve what I was advising. I also realised that I was repeating a second piece of advice, 'an evaluation needs to be a document you can act on, not just a record for an evidence folder'. So, the five minute lesson evaluation was born!

My idea was for the evaluation to be used in conjunction with the five minute lesson plan (see Idea 9). It needed to have a similar format and it required simple steps. How it works:

- Were the lesson objectives met?
- How did the starter activity develop? Was it successful?
- How did the students know their starting and ending points? What evidence can you provide?
- What learning experiences worked? Why? What will you change?
- Differentiation: What worked/what didn't work? Why? What next?
- Assessment for Learning (AfL): How did you assess the progress?
- Can you evaluate the student outcomes?
- What will you do differently next time?

#5MinEval

by @IanMcDaid

#Stickability

"What's brown and sticky? A stick!"

Insist that students leave your classroom taking away what you need them to bring back.

Think about when you're teaching a series of lessons, one today, one tomorrow, one the following day. What should students bring back with them? When you ask students to recall prior knowledge, what do you expect them to say? This is stickability.

Use the two ideas below to make your lessons sticky!

1 As students leave your classroom give them a secret object to reinforce learning. Challenge students to utilise this object in their homework or to return to class and reference the object in the next lesson's objectives.
2 Create a sticky pad or board on your classroom door. Students pull off one Post-it note or object as they leave. This can be as simple as a keyword with a definition; or an activity they need to complete and upload online to win a prize!

Further reading can be found online at www.bloomsbury.com/TeacherToolkit

Teaching tip

Think about how you could use #Stickability to evidence progress in an observation. If you were an observer, what would you look for to evidence progress from start to finish? How could you evidence progress over a half term, without using grades or levels?

Taking it further

Make stickability live up to its name! Choose a student volunteer to stand up in front of the class. Use clothes pegs or Post-it notes to record key learning takeaways from students. Students stick their ideas to a physical part of the body, such as a school jumper or forearm. You will hopefully be left with a few important beads of knowledge sticking, along with the sound of laughter resonating.

#Stickability

Failsafe strategies

Part 12

Shush – the deadly sin

"Tackling low level behaviour without saying shush!"

By using alternative words and phrases for 'shush' we can reinforce vocabulary growth in our students but also avoid using persistent negative reinforcement to control low level behaviour.

Over the years, I've developed an aversion to the verb, 'shush' or 'sssh'. This has mainly stemmed from observing other teachers in assemblies, tutor time and in lessons where behaviour has been far from good. Now, you may argue, that I've got better things to do that focus on something so petty, but let me explain why.

It starts with Unconditional Positive Regard (UPR), a concept first brought to my attention in Hywel Roberts' book, '*Oops! Helping Children Learn Accidentally*'. The term was devised by the psychologist Carl Rogers and it describes how children should be exposed to UPR, irrespective of their actions. Carl Rogers believed that UPR is essential to healthy development. Children who are not exposed to UPR may come to see themselves in negative ways. UPR can help children to accept responsibility for themselves.

The word 'shush' is often used to control low level behaviour. It is a common occurrence when punishing students and it usually has negative connotations.

By removing 'shush' from your vocabulary you remove one of the persistent negative reinforcers from your teaching.

Shush is a deadly sin! I challenge you to find an alternative the next time you hear yourself saying 'sssh'.

Bonus idea ★

Consider implementing speaking levels in your classroom and inform your students of the acceptable noise level for each of your activities. For example:

Volume 0 = No talking, individual, silent working.

Volume 1 = Whispering in pairs.

Volume 2 = Small group discussions.

Volume 3 = Whole class discussions.

Volume 4 = Louder than normal, so that 'fun learning' can be heard.

Rehearse the different levels with your class and remind them of the number they should be working at regularly.

#Shush

Tough love

"I love you but I cannot smile today."

Try to breakdown the barriers to learning. Consider using the 'I Love You' game in your lessons for some fun, or even in tougher situations.

Get to know your students; every single one of them. This will be your greatest success in any classroom throughout your career. If you understand every student, even a snapshot about their life, then I can guarantee that you will be a well-respected teacher and ideas like this one will be a breeze.

The 'I Love You' game has worked for me for over 13 years, especially as a form tutor. I've even used it as a senior teacher when dealing with students on a Friday night in senior detention and with those facing exclusion. It can be hard to implement across a whole class, but with a bit of time and effort it works! Play the 'I Love You' game with the following dialogue, and watch how hard it is not to smile!

Teacher: I love you Noah, but I cannot smile today.
Noah: I love you too Miss, but I won't smile today.

Now crank this humble game up to the next level:
Teacher: I love you Noah. I love (this) about your work, but I cannot smile today.
Noah: I love you too Miss. To love this work more, I need to do (this), but I won't smile today.

Teaching tip

The 'I Love You' game, 'Two Stars and a Wish' or 'A Kiss and Two Kicks' are all great ways of getting students to praise and critique each others' work and to accept praise and criticism from others.

Taking it further

Get students to play the 'I Love You' game peer to peer:

Noah: I love you Rohana. I love (this) about your work, but I cannot smile today.

Roshana: I love you too Noah. To love this work more, I need to do (this), but I won't smile today.

MINT

"Stay in MINT condition."

Use the foolproof MINT strategy to ensure all instructions are delivered with clarity and in bite-sized chunks, and you'll never hear 'I don't know what to do' ever again!

No matter what point in the lesson you are at, whether starting, packing away, or introducing a secondary aspect to a lesson, providing students with MINT instructions will remove any pestiferous 'what do I need to do?' questions from your classroom. Here's how MINT works:

M= Materials: This simply means the resources to be used. Do not over-complicate things. For example: 'A3 paper; a pencil and ruler; the A5 worksheet.'

I = In or out of seats: Be explicit about this for every activity. For example 'You will be working out of your seats, around the classroom visiting various sources.'

N = Noise level: Be clear about the accepted volume. You could use the scale from Idea 88). For example 'The noise level is quiet conversations in groups'.

T = Time: Specify clearly the time needed to complete the activity, including the last warning and completion time: For example 'the time for you to do this is seven minutes. I will give you a final one minute warning.'

KISS

"Keep It Simple, Stupid!"

Most systems work best if they are kept simple. Simplicity should always be a key goal especially when giving instructions to students.

KISS, an acronym for Keep It Simple, Stupid, is a design principle noted by the U.S. Navy in 1960. The KISS principle states that simplicity should be a primary aim for all designs and unnecessary complexity should be avoided. This principle naturally started to embed itself into all my teaching styles and all the subjects I have taught over the years, from the teaching of Art, Food Technology and Product Design, to History, ICT and Electronics. Use this simple strategy to inform all your teaching strategies and student management.

Teaching tip

Choose a time and place to use KISS. It works very well with starter activities and demonstrations throughout the lesson.

- **Keep** all instructions brief!
- **It** only needs to be one or two minutes, listing key reminders and materials needed.
- **Simple** instructions can be offered in bitesize pieces.
- **Stupid** diversions can often lead to misunderstanding and repeating of the process.

My five top tips for what *not* to do:

1 Asking for clarification from a student makes KISS superfluous.
2 Opening the floor for questioning.
3 At the start, talking about what you will do at the end of the lesson!
4 Jumping ahead of yourself. For example, listing all the resources needed for a task, even though only one or two sources will be needed immediately.
5 Waffling on and on and on...

(#KISS)

Four-by-four

"A golden oldie from the Key Stage Three national strategy."

Group your students into fours for this drafting and redrafting idea.

This technique can be applied to all classroom situations, for example, a performance in Drama, classwork such as a drawing or spoken poem, a throwing technique demonstrated in P.E. or pronunciation practice in Spanish. Through embedding this strategy, learners can develop confidence in assessing and critiquing their own and others' work and become adept at setting meaningful targets for improvement.

- Students are paired up in groups of four and each stage below is rotated to each member.
- Stage One: Student One (all students individually) attempts the task for five or ten minutes.
- The teacher provides criteria, which are presented to the class to be used to assess the work.
- Stage Two: Student Two is asked to assess and develop the piece of work created by Student One. This means, all students complete the work by rotating their original work to the next student on the table.
- Stage Three: Student Three offers feedback to Student One and Student Two, before attempting another redraft of the work.
- Stage Four: Student Four prepares a final redraft of the work created by Student One and modified by Students Two and Three, before presenting the completed and developed works to the group or class.
- The work is returned to the original source for review and action.

Stay composed

"Let's face it, if you're not composed, you're hardly likely to be cutting the grade in the classroom!"

Stay calm and collected: challenge your students to talk in whispers throughout the entire plenary.

Over the years, I have identified the factors that get my blood boiling and the best ways to calm myself down. The suggestions below are focused on composure techniques linked to classroom practice.

Factors:

- Expecting a difficult class.
- Work pressure and deadlines.
- The expectation to go above and beyond and complete work in your own time.
- Poor diet and too many school dinners.
- Late nights.
- Working 50-60 hour weeks, every week, all year.

Solutions:

- Focus your energies on starting lessons off well and ending on a gentle and calm note.
- Reduce coffee and tea intake.
- Place a large bottle of water on your desk.
- Get to bed early. Before ten o'clock at least once during the weekend.
- Switch off for at least one day at the weekend, every weekend.
- Turn the email alerts off your mobile device.
- Speak to your well-being officer at school. Don't have one? Ask your headteacher today!

Teaching tip

Create or join a group at your school that aims to ensure composed teaching and learning. Take a look at this Teachers TV video I worked on to reduce teacher pressures with my staff: www.bit.ly/StaffWellBeing.

Taking it further

Join a gym or start an evening class. Commit one night a week to doing something outside of work, that you enjoy and most importantly, helps you switch off. This will help you to become more composed during the day.

Bonus idea

Learn to say 'no' at work and at home. Just try it!

Abstract ideas

Part 13

NO EXCUSES!

"A motto to establish an ethos for outstanding."

A simple expectation; make it the mantra for your classroom.

I once came across the words NO EXCUSES emblazoned two metres high across a large wall in a school playground. By not allowing your students to ply you with excuses about forgotten homework, or reasons for being late to class, you cut out an awful lot of time wasting and begin to cultivate an ethos of outstanding teaching and learning. I now have my own NO EXCUSES sign in my classroom and one glued to the back of my planner. It's constantly on show as a reminder of the ethos.

For every new class I teach I create my own three straightforward beliefs, which are established from the outset, and NO EXCUSES is one of those three non-negotiables in any classroom, every year. NO EXCUSES is not sold as a classroom rule, it is sold as an expectation with a much more positive spin.

This philosophy is further strengthened by a simply analogy. High expectations are the minimum. I want students in my care to *exceed* my expectations. Repeat the expectation to the class three times and you are soon on your way to a NO EXCUSES ethos. You can then refer to the sign with a simple finger point, without even moving your lips, which will nip the student excuse in the bud (and sometimes raise a smile)!

Teaching tip

Eat, sleep, drink and teach NO EXCUSES in everything you do. NO EXCUSES applies to you too! Practise what you preach! Ensure that it becomes a philosophy, not a reactionary tool for rebuffing incomplete homework.

Taking it further

NO EXCUSES can also form part of a class discussion. For example, by agreeing together what the NO EXCUSES philosophy criteria are and displaying the non-negotiables on the wall. Students will feel they have ownership and soon be examining you to keep to the criteria.

#NoExcuses

Shut Up!

"Nah, shut up man!"

Make a huge (I mean MASSIVE) classroom sign banning unproductive and disrespectful language!

The Outstanding criteria suggest that 'students make every effort to ensure that others learn and thrive in an atmosphere of respect and dignity.'

'Shut up!' is another one of my classroom mantras. It can be applied to suit the context of your own behavioural systems, or simply used as a common moral code of practice. I've found that my students are very good at telling each other to 'shut up!' so as a result, I banned the use of the word in my classroom. You can adapt this idea to any school or playground terminology, whatever the need may be, to ensure lessons continue without interruption and that students 'make every effort to ensure that others learn and thrive in an atmosphere of respect and dignity.'

- Inform your students why standards of vocabulary and respect for each other have to be maintained.
- Use a credit and debit system for rewarding and punishing behaviour. Every time a student uses a disrespectful word, they receive a debit. (In my school this is so effective that now they apologise to me and their fellow students in the playground!)
- Accentuate the positive. Offer a reward for positive phrases or keywords that can be regularly used in a lesson. For example, 'can I offer this solution?' You could offer bonus points for extra creative phrases!

#ShutUp!

Message in a bottle

"The class were so enthused by the lesson that they forgot to leave at the end of the day!"

Create a map of your classroom with sequential clues dotted around to aid the learning.

Aim for consistently high student engagement that leads to rapid progress and better learning. What strategies do you use to increase student engagement? Can you do this at any point of the lesson, time and time again? How do you do it? Engagement strategies can include all types of incentive. Below are some quick wins:

1 Place a message in a clear glass bottle. This message could contain simple answers for a Maths test or the solutions and suggestions to a long-term research project. Consider handwriting the answers and then in the lesson, folding the paper up and sealing the bottle, or you could print off an email from a collaborative classroom and roll it up and place inside.

2 Inform your students that what you are about to tell them is confidential.

3 Whisper. Use exaggerated facial expressions combined with slow and engaging hand and body movement.

4 Get the whole class standing up on the tables, *Dead Poets Society* style! That means you too!

5 Write the answers to your lesson plan questions on a set of cards and place them in a sealed envelope. Emblazon the outside with the words TOP SECRET.

Teaching tip

Take a moment to think about all the things you wanted as a child including the things your parents wouldn't allow you to have and implement these ideas into your lesson plans. For example, a simple reward each lesson could lead to a greater end of term reward. Some great ideas I've seen in schools include bicycles on the walls and iPods displayed in cabinets for all students to see!

Bonus idea ★

Create a vlog (video log) of secrets that you can replay to the class revealing information each time groups of students unearth information. These vlogs could also include other teachers from your school revealing information, adding cross-curricular content into your lesson.

Test your strength

"Come and have a go if you think you're hard enough!"

Photocopy this page and share it with a colleague. Have a race to complete all 20 tasks.

Teaching tip

Do not set any detentions for the entire day. No matter what! Resolve the issues in other ways. Be creative.

Think you're a good teacher? Even stretch to say you're outstanding? Do you have enough bravado to consider being deprived of key resources and strategies that you use everyday? Here's an abstract and relatively risky idea for you to try. I've listed a number of ideas for you to test your strength. Quiz yourself by setting yourself and your colleagues some of the following tasks. I bet you can't complete the list in less than three weeks! Please tweet me if you do!

Test your strength ideas:

1 **A surprisingly strong idea** My students don't need any objectives today!
2 What interactive whiteboard? You won't see me using one.
3 Drop all of your class rules for one lesson.
4 Turn off all the classroom computers!
5 No paper allowed.
6 The students will teach the starter activity in each lesson today.
7 My students will evaluate my lesson.
8 Post-it notes are banned for the week.
9 Keep your classroom door open all day!
10 **A great idea** No PowerPoint presentations for the entire week!
11 Avoid the following words: right, okay, listen, now, quiet, shush, move.
12 Do not use a green or red pen.
13 Mini whiteboards. Keep them out of sight.

14 Stand up. Yes, you! You are not allowed to sit down for the entire lesson.

15 Push all the chairs and desks to the outside walls and sit on the floor in a circle.

16 Worksheets. Not today. Not even for the whole week.

17 In this lesson, levels and grades are not to be discussed.

18 Invite two teachers into your lesson to observe you completing task 5, 7, 11 or 15.

19 The sink. It's out of bounds for the day! Do not turn on those taps Art teachers.

20 Plan for your Teaching Assistant to deliver 15 minutes of the lesson.

Tick off the ideas and note down the date when you completed them.

Bonus idea

Why not set a challenge within your department and ask colleagues to complete three or four 'test your strength' suggestions in just one day! This will guarantee all students walking into your department will be receiving risk-taking lessons for the entire day. Fantastic!

#StrongTeacher

Bums on seats

"An alternative approach to seating plans."

Take a photograph of your students sitting in your classroom now, then read on.

I came across this idea after sending a colleague off to a training event. She handed me a seating plan, but it was no ordinary seating plan. It was a photograph of a classroom with real students sitting around the room. The visual representation of the plan was striking. Immediately I could match student names to faces. It was more than a two dimensional version with table layouts, it was the classroom itself in action.

I imagined myself standing in the position of the camera, lesson planning or observing the students, looking at where each student was sitting. What made this seating plan have that extra touch of gravitas was that it included prior and current data. There were colour coded sections with abbreviations and all of the required context needed for lesson planning and classroom observations, for example, which students are gifted and talented, who receives free school meals, and individual grade predictions.

- Get into a position where you can see all your students in their seats and take a photo. Imagine where an observer would sit. If you can't fit all the students in one photo take a couple and try to join them up.
- Upload the photo to a computer.
- Add any relevant data next to each student by pen or digitally.
- You could include latest assessment grades, effort, or the last time you called home. Be creative!

#Bummer

Blender

"Imagine mixing it all up!"

Cut up your lesson plan into various sections, with timings, and place each of them into a hat. Allow students to pick out a section at random. Once picked, that's what you teach!

Research in the past couple of decades has begun to use the term 'blended learning'. Blended learning is a recognised education programme in which a student learns through at least three key methods: Online learning, Mobile learning and Classroom learning.

The online delivery content has some element of student control. Students are still expected to attend a breeze block school structure and enter a face-to-face classroom but this experience is blended with online and mobile environments. This means that learning can take place outside the traditional classroom location, outside the traditional classroom timeframe and also outside the traditional classroom pathway.

Some of us are becoming familiar with virtual learning platforms, mobile devices and how they link in with day-to-day teaching, however, the vast majority are still far behind. Technology is a growing part of our lives, and more importantly, of our students' lives. The opportunities for learning online are vast and they are just waiting to be discovered.

The top three benefits of 'blended learning' are:

1 The opportunity for data collection and reporting.
2 To inform teacher-instruction and learning.
3 Students have greater control over their learning.

Teaching tip

Follow this link to read a more detailed research piece called 'Blended Learning' by Staker and Horn, May 2012: www.bit.ly/IWantToKnowMoreNow.

Taking it further

The best known expert is Mr. Salman Khan, whose Khan Academy (www.khanacademy.org/) contains a huge library of video content across all subject areas and levels. The Khan Academy hosts over five million unique users and about 15,000 different classrooms use Mr. Khan's lessons as part of their regular instruction every month!

#Blender

Twitter for the classroom #GetMeStarted

"Welcome to the Twittersphere!"

Set up your own Twitter account; share your experiences and reflect on outstanding!

I started using Twitter in the classroom in 2010, using the account @Ask_Mr_McGill. It was a fantastic revision tool for my Sixth Form students. Gradually the success started spreading across the school and beyond. Now I share my teaching tips and experience with over 27,000 followers(!) from no less than six separate accounts.

How to get started:

1. Understand Twitter before creating an account for professional or classroom purposes.
2. Define the purpose of your account. Will it be for one class, or a general account for all ages and lesson interaction?
3. What will you use it for? Setting homework, sharing photos, revision?
4. Lock down your account.
5. Share your Twitter handle (username) with your students.
6. Spend some time teaching your students how Twitter works. Ask them to follow your account but insist that you will not follow back. This is generally useful and sound ICT practice for safeguarding.

7 Consider a unique hashtag with enables text vocabulary to become an interactive search engine within each message. I created #AskMcGill. In layman's terms, this means that anyone can follow the conversation by clicking on and following the hashtag #AskMcGill.
8 Start small. Get all your students logged on and get them following you and your account. Then ask them to share what they are learning in their first tweet. Make sure they include the same hashtag for everyone to follow the chat.
9 Demonstrate how all the messages in the conversation can be viewed by searching for a hashtag.
10 Archive the conversation as evidence of learning using www.scribd.com. You can print it off or share it digitally.

There is a wealth of information here from @Edudemic: www.bit.ly/Edudemic and Andy Lewis, @TalkingDonkeyRE also has some great practical advice for class teachers who blog. Alternatively, if you want to introduce a colleague to Twitter, try @BATTUK (Bring A Teacher To Twitter).

Do remember that students must be aged 13 or over to use Twitter, so this is an idea better used with your older students.

Taking it further

Consider sharing your classroom tweets via a blog, popular ones are Edmodo, Blogger or Wordpress. This information can be used as a channel to communicate with parents and the rest of the school. Check your ICT policy in your school beforehand.

#GetMeStarted